Norman Duchesneau has worked in law enforcement since he was 19 years old. His career has wound its way through many roles: call taker, cadet, patrolman, investigator, detective, and trainer. Of all of these, he is most proud to have been a patrolman because it was that role where he was able to affect the most lives, and believes that he helped the most people. It is also where he has had the most fun.

He loves his family and pets, and credits his wife, Michelle, with much of his success. "It is because she believes in me that I find the courage to do what I do," he often says.

Norman is a nerd and wears that badge as proudly as his police badge. He loves comics and superheroes—Batman most specifically. His on-going love of Tabletop RPGs has lasted longer that his career. It started before and if he has any say in the matter will continue beyond. He still works the streets, and if it is late at night, when you read this, he may well be patrolling his city now. He hopes you laugh as you read this. He does love to get a laugh.

To Michelle, the best wife a man could hope for and my constant inspiration.

Norman Duchesneau

NECESSARY CHANCES

30 Years of Law Enforcement Stories as Told
by a Smart Ass

AUSTIN MACAULEY PUBLISHERS™
LONDON • CAMBRIDGE • NEW YORK • SHARJAH

Ordering Information:
Quantity sales: special discounts are available on quantity purchases by corporations, associations, and others. For details, contact the publisher at the address below.

Publisher's Cataloging-in-Publication data
Duchesneau, Norman
Necessary Chances

ISBN 9781641826891 (Paperback)
ISBN 9781641826907 (Hardback)
ISBN 9781645364627 (ePub e-book)

The main category of the book — BIOGRAPHY & AUTOBIOGRAPHY / Law Enforcement

Library of Congress Control Number: 2019907818

www.austinmacauley.com/us

First Published (2019)
Austin Macauley Publishers LLC
40 Wall Street, 28th Floor
New York, NY 10005
USA

mail-usa@austinmacauley.com
+1 (646) 5125767

The writing of this book has been inspired by far more people than I could hope to name. It certainly would not have been possible without the love and support of my beautiful wife. My brother, who is far more talented and creative than me, has shown me that there is truly only one way to fail, and that is to not try. My brother and sister are officers who have had my back and listened to my stories for decades, these are people who have hopefully learned from me (both from my successes and my failures) and are people that I have learned from and continue to learn from every day. My small circle of very dear and brilliant friends, who have repeatedly said to me, "You should write a book." To them, I say, "Hey look, I wrote a book."

I would specifically like to mention David. David is a clerk at a convenience store where I very often get my coffee at the beginning of my shift. Seeing him three to four times a week has led us to have many deep and philosophical conversations. Okay, maybe not deep and philosophical but conversations nonetheless. One night, many years ago, as I was walking out the door, David said something that stuck in my head. As I opened the door, he said, "Good night, Officer. Don't take any unnecessary chances."

On a whim I replied, "Unfortunately, sir, they are all necessary."

Police officers are a rather suspicious bunch, and because the night he said that to me went rather smoothly, I now insist that he says it every time I see him. It's kind of like a baseball player who must touch the door jam on his way to the field.

When I told David I was starting a book, he would constantly ask how I was doing and he would say, "A writer writes."

David, my friend...I wrote.

Start with a Joke
(A Good Joke)

My smart mouth, and urge to make a joke, has not been restricted to my time on the streets. Each year all officers have to attend a week of what is known as in-service training. This is usually conducted over several days and contains several standard classes, such as legal update, traffic law update, first aid/CPR, and defensive tactics. Each year a random topic is also added. On occasion, they have been informative and interesting. Mostly, they're schlepped together and pitiful. The classroom is a perfect environment for a smart mouth like me, especially when it's a classroom full of bored cops. I do love a captive audience.

One year, a woman was brought in to speak on the subject of race relations. This was a long time ago, before the Rodney King incident, and things were not so tense. The woman giving the class was of Cape Verdean descent. For those of you who don't know, it is an island off the coast of Africa. It has been colonized by many countries, but most of the people are a mix of African and Portuguese. They tend to have a caramel complexion. They tend to speak a version of Portuguese. Almost exclusively, they do not consider themselves black.

Someone must have told this woman to start her class with a joke. They neglected, however, to tell her to start with a *'good'* joke. I was seated in front of the class directly in front

9

of the podium. I could easily see that she was nervous. She fidgeted with her hands and her eyes darted along the back wall rather than make eye contact with the 20 or so alpha males in front of her. The fact that she was a beautiful woman, wearing a tight skirt and a low-cut blouse led to some of the men leering at her like a starving wolf stares at the lamb. I'm sure that this added to her anxiety. The following paragraph contains the 'joke' she chose to open her race relations class with.

"God was baking cookies. The first batch He burnt and that was the blacks. The second batch He underdid and that's the whites. His third batch came out a perfect golden brown and that was the Cape Verdean's."

She was treated with a deafening silence, as none of us knew exactly how to react to this somewhat ridiculous attempt at a joke. I couldn't help myself; I raised my hand, and she nodded to me. This was her second mistake of the day.

"But what if He was out to make dark chocolate fudge? Then, you are underdone too. If He were out to make vanilla wafers, then you are burnt as well. And if He were out to make mint chocolate chip, we are all pretty much screwed. Not to mention you completely left the Asians out of the baking equation."

Yes, I agree, I was mean and unfair to the young, inexperienced teacher, but I got my laugh, and really, that's all I was looking for. To her credit, she continued on with her class and seemed rather unflustered by my interruption. About 45 minutes into the class, she decided it was time for some role-play. She also decided that since I had embarrassed her, she would attempt embarrassing me (Really, embarrass me? Like that could possibly happen). She moved a chair to the front of the room and had me sit facing the class. She informed me that I was going to mimic going to a call. She informed me that the call notes were that there was a group of minorities disturbing. She told me to grab the imaginary steering wheel and drive to the call. I did her one better and buckled my seatbelt first. I then began to mimic driving to the call. I turned my imaginary steering wheel. I used my imaginary directional. She asked me, "What about the sirens?" I told her that I work midnights and never use them. I hit the brakes. I attempted to exit the car, remembered my seatbelt, unhooked it, and stood up. She stopped me and asked me what I was doing. I told her I was going to quell the disturbance. She asked me what type of disturbance I was going to.

I repeated what she said, "A group of minorities disturbing."

She replied, "Ah, but what kind of minority?"

I now perceived what I believe to be her intention here. By asking me what type of minority I was approaching, she hoped to show that I had an innate prejudicial idea of what minority was. Had I said 'Blacks,' 'Latinos,' or 'Cape Verdean,' she could show that that was my innate thought of what a minority was. I couldn't let this happen and I thought quickly.

"Epileptic dwarves with a prosthesis," I replied.

She looked at me in complete shock and said, "What?" A series of snickers and stifled laughs spread through the room but was quickly shut down by a glare from this now truly flustered woman. She looked at me again and asked, "What do you mean?"

I replied, "Dwarves, you know, little people, who happen to have epilepsy and are missing a limb that has been replaced by a prosthesis. There can't be more than four or five on the entire planet. They're having a small get together. They've gotten a little loud." I then turned away from her and waved to my imaginary disturbance, "Hey, fellas, we've had some

11

complaints. Do you think you could try and keep it down?" I then sat back down in my chair/car, reattached my seatbelt, and drove away. She hustled to the table, handed me all the paperwork she had planned to hand out for the day, and told me I was excused.

Never Double Denim

Not every instance throughout my career has been a stunning victory. Not every case has been funny. Some only became funny after time and distance have made them so. There is a saying, and I don't know to whom I should credit it but I have found it to be true.

'The essence of comedy is tragedy plus time.'

What follows is a story that at the time seemed quite tragic to me, but as decades have passed, I now see the humor in it and happily tell it to friends at parties.

A large supermarket in my city, one that is part of a national chain, used to hire paid detail officers to assist with shoplifter control. The job has varied over the years, but at the time, it was a plain-clothed, undercover assignment. The officer's job was to walk around the store in an attempt to arrest shoplifters in the act. On the night in which the story takes place, I was dressed in jeans with motorcycle boots. I also wore an old concert shirt and a denim jacket. (I know, double denim is a fashion sin; I was young and foolish.) Poor weather coupled with the fact that it was less than an hour till closing left the store almost empty. Having no one in the store to watch, I chose to stand by a magazine rack and pass the time. I had picked a fitness magazine with a focus on bodybuilding.

Anyone who knows me knows that my interest in this subject never actually extended beyond the reading stage. Now, you can picture the scene, a young man in his 20s, with a military style haircut and the aforementioned double denim, standing alone in a supermarket, reading a muscle magazine.

A middle-aged man walked into the store, and I sighed, thinking that I now had to keep an eye on him and put away the article I was reading. The man rectified my dilemma as he walked up to the magazine rack and stood close by me. I was thinking that keeping an eye on this gentleman was going to be rather easy. The man picked up the exact same magazine that I was reading. Well, not the exact magazine but a copy of the same issue. He began to page through it, and I went back to reading my article. Every few minutes, this man would point out a photo of some bodybuilder in the magazine and ask my opinion as to how a well-developed one set of muscles or another was. I would glance casually and agree with him as to whatever opinion he had about the bodybuilders he was pointing out. With age and experience, I now know I should've suspected something, but my youth and *naïveté* played against me.

While reading the last bits of my article, I felt something I had never expected. The gentleman standing next to me had reached down with his right hand and was now holding and fondling my groin. To be perfectly blunt, the man had a firm grasp on my dick. I reacted quickly, grabbing the man's wrist, straightening his elbow, and slamming him to the ground. Before he realized what was happening, I had him cuffed up. I screamed, "You're under arrest!" I would like to think I sounded professional and forceful; the reality is I probably sounded like a scared high school girl. I pulled out my concealed radio and called for assistance. It was at that moment that I realized my monumental mistake.

Two senior officers arrived to assist me as I walked my defendant out of the store. They volunteered to take the man to booking and start the process for me. They then asked me what the charge was, and I realized that the laughter was going to start here and not end for years.

"Indecent assault and battery," I replied, almost in a mumble.

"Really? Wow! Who's the victim, one of the clerks?" the older man asked, genuinely excited about such a serious charge stemming from such a mundane detail.

After some hesitation and trying to find some way out of it, I was forced to answer that the victim was in fact me. I laugh about it now but nowhere near as loud and long as those men laughed about it then.

Tools of the Trade

I'm not sure if it is just pure luck, or if it is because I am rather quick-witted and an even faster talker, but in my long career—which has touched four different decades—I have very seldom had to use any of the tools on my belt. In fact, in all that time, I have never had to ball up my fist and hit a man. I have made limited use of my pepper spray and even less of my Taser. This is not to say that I'm opposed to using these tools. I think they are fantastic tools, and they have served me very well in the few times that I have used them. My first instinct is to attempt to talk someone down rather than fight them down. If talking fails, my hands on approach has always been to grapple my opponent to the ground and bend them into the position I need them to be in. I have been lucky in that this technique has worked more than 90% of the time. This is not to indicate that I have not used the tools on my belt; like I said, when I have needed them, they have served me well.

One night while responding to a domestic disturbance, I was assisting two very young rookie officers who were to be primary on the call. Upon arriving at the indicated intersection, we found a young man in his early 20s who was absolutely outraged. He was a black male standing a little over six feet tall. He had a large build, more like that of a linebacker than that of a running back. That is to say, he was a large man but not overly muscular. He was walking in a tight circle in the center of the quiet intersection, occasionally punching a street sign or kicking a fire hydrant. Multiple attempts to communicate with him seemed futile. When he did not respond to us with nonsensical grunts, he would only say that he was too mad to talk. We gave this about ten minutes, hoping that he would tire himself, or at the very least, talk himself down. Unfortunately, the opposite seemed to be happening. He had more the look of a man psyching himself up for a big game than that of a man working through his problems.

The rookies and I held back and continued to attempt to verbally talk him down. Soon after his 10th or 12th lap around the tight circle—he was walking—this furious man began to take off his shirt. The removal of a hat or a shirt is very often an indicator that a fight is about to commence. The rookies showed me that they knew this as they took that opportunity to move in on the man while his vision was obscured by the removal of his shirt. I held the young officers back however and removed the pepper spray from my belt. As the shirt cleared the man's face, I wet his face down with the pepper spray. The effect was perfect and instantaneous. He fell to his knees, screaming and crying and begging for any relief. He immediately became not only intelligible but exceptionally apologetic. He was taken into custody without further incident. Once at booking, we were able to flush his face out with water, and he became one of the most polite and cooperative prisoners I have ever dealt with.

One night, I along with several other officers was called to the hospital, specifically the secure holding section. The call notes indicated that hospital security was requesting assistance with an out-of-control patient. I arrived almost simultaneously

17

with three other officers. The first site that I saw upon entering the area was an older security officer desperately trying to hold a door closed. This man was older, probably in his early 50s; he was tall and lean with graying hair and he had a look of fear and desperation on his face. Looking through the thin window of the door the security officer was desperately trying to hold closed, was a young man in his underwear. This young man was black with a shaved head and a lean muscular build. He was using the rolling table, used to feed patients, as a battering ram. His violent efforts had so far cracked the door and he was approximately four or five good strikes away from breaking it entirely and setting himself free. As I looked in the door, our eyes met, and the man very earnestly implored me to shoot him. I pulled out my Taser and removed the cartridge so that I could display the tool's arc and remind him of its capacity.

"Do it! Do it! Do it!" was the man's only response.

I had the other officers stack up behind me as I replaced the cartridge to the front of my Taser so that I could employ the prongs. I then instructed the security officer to release the door and step back. He did so, and as he did, the door flung open, and I deployed the Taser. The result was instantaneous. The prongs shot forward and embedded in the man, one in his chest, the other just above his hip. He went immediately rigid and fell to the floor. The other officers and the security officer stood stunned. When the Taser is employed, the subject is incapacitated for about five seconds. Once those five seconds have expired, the officer who deployed the Taser has to either pull the trigger again to start another five-second run or the subject has to be restrained. Not wanting to employ a second time, I yelled:

"Somebody cuff him!"

My shout seemed to wake everyone up, and the man was quickly handcuffed. The jolt to his system appeared to wake him up as well as it brought an end to his ranting, and he became very cooperative and almost conversational instantaneously.

Men Don't Scare Me,
Babies Do

I was 23 years old when I became a police officer. Specifically, I turned 23 years old midway through the Academy. I did not have a vast life experience before my service as a policeman, and there are some things that the Academy simply does not prepare you for. Among these things: the disdain many people have for the police, the mind-numbing ignorance of some people, the variety of ways people find to hurt themselves or others, and dealing with babies…specifically birth.

On a cold winter's night, with snow falling, during my first year on the job, I was working alone, that is to say in a one-man car. I was sent to a medic call, and the notes of the call were vague at best. The dispatcher cited, "Language problems," as the cause of the lack of information. I remember arriving on the scene and hearing the medics on the radio state that they were en route from the hospital. That meant that I was going to be alone on the scene for several minutes. I grabbed the medic bag out of my car and headed into the house with all the confidence that I could muster. That confidence left me very quickly. The first sight that I saw upon entering the apartment stopped me in my tracks.

You know when you see something that is so out of place that your mind has trouble registering it and it takes a few moments for you to process? Well, this was one of those situations.

Lying on a sofa, her head away and feet towards me, was a woman. Her knees were up, her legs were splayed, and between her legs, I saw something I just didn't recognize. The situation was she was giving birth and crowning. For those of you who don't know, 'crowning' means the baby has made its way to the exit. What I was seeing was this woman's vagina spread wide by the baby's head making its way out. A quick glance around the room did nothing to soothe my mind. Seated on another sofa across the room were this woman's three other children. (The previous is not a typo, three children watching.) The father was walking in a very tight circle between the two sofas. It is very safe to say that in a competition for which of us looked most frightened, the father won. I was in second place, and rapidly gaining on him. The lady giving birth may have also been scared, but I believe the pain was covering up that emotion nicely. Adding to the chaos of the situation, there were only two people in the room who spoke English, me and the oldest child on the sofa, a young boy of about six years old. Through him I got the father to sit down and take deep breaths. In dealing with the woman giving birth, I just relied on soft, soothing noises.

By the time I got my gloves on, informed dispatch of my situation, and prepared some trauma pads, the baby's entire head and one shoulder were out. My wife often asks me how I can stay so calm in a variety of situations. I always tell her that once you have seen a screaming, blood-covered human head sticking out of a vagina, everything else seems rather vanilla. Steadying myself, I did my very best to recall my training. There wasn't much. I did remember the instructor telling me, or rather the class, that we should not 'try to stick the baby

21

back in.' So my first instinct was not going to work. I then remembered that once one shoulder was out, you should turn the baby so that the shoulders are pointing up and down. I also remembered that there is a phenomenon that is common to women who have had multiple children. That term is called **'explosive child birth.'**

In my humble opinion, there is no more apt term in the universe than '**explosive child birth**.' I moved that tiny little shoulder less than a quarter of an inch, and the child and all the ichors behind it splashed out and into my hands. The baby was crying. The mother was crying. The father was crying. I think I might've been crying. The children on the sofa seemed rather at ease. In a panic and really not knowing what to do, I lifted the mother's housecoat to expose her chest and place the baby upon her. I took the sterile trauma pads and applied them to the infant and had the mother hold the whole package. The laborious part being over, I attempted to recall more training. I did not have much success.

I did recall somewhere, someone saying that once the child is born, you should feel the umbilical cord. If the cord is still pulsing, everything is okay. If however, the cord stops pulsing, you must tie it off. I'm not sure, but I think it has something to do with the baby draining back out. So there I was holding on to a slimy cord that led from the baby back into the hole it just came from, feeling for a pulse. I felt one and I was elated. I called, asking for the medics' estimated arrival time. I hoped I sounded relaxed and confident. I know for a fact I failed in that endeavor entirely. As the pulse in the cord became fainter, it became harder to tell. As the baby's umbilical pulse faded, mine raced out of control. With my free hand, I began to unlace one of my boots, intending to use the bootlace to tie off the cord. At that moment, the EMTs arrived, and I practically fainted. They took over; I sat down.

The baby was a little girl (no chance they'll name it after me) and her birth and health were perfectly normal. Well, normal except that the birth was assisted by rookie officer scared out of his mind and to be perfectly honest, 'faking it.' After several years, I lost track of the family, but I can say with certainty that that young girl made it to her 18th birthday healthy, bright, and happy.

Thank You All for Serving

Just before I started working at the police department as a call taker/dispatcher, I joined the Army National Guard. I spent 13 weeks at Fort Benning Georgia, completing basic and advanced training as an infantry soldier. In total, I served 30 years in the Army National Guard. I attained the rank of Staff Sergeant, and have a strong dedication to the non-commissioned officer corps. I am very proud of my service and I am very proud of anyone who has also chosen to serve. Be it army, marine corps, navy, or air force, I am proud of my brothers and sisters in uniform. This, of course, does not mean that every encounter I've had with servicemen and women has been positive.

For a period of time, there was a large Coast Guard cutter docked in my city. The crew of this cutter would often be seen out and about in the downtown area. One morning, at about 2 o'clock, just after the bars closed, I was driving through the area in what was one of the most torrential downpours I had ever seen. I observed a few figures dressed in white walking along a roadway that led into the downtown area proper. As I got closer, I noticed that these four characters were from the Coast Guard and by my estimation had about 2 miles walk ahead of them to get back to their cutter. I pulled over and asked if they were enlisted or officers. The three men who were walking explained that they were all noncommissioned officers, and that the female who accompanied them was an officer. I explained that I was a noncommissioned officer and would give the enlisted men a ride back to the cutter. To her credit, the officer took this in stride and continued her walk as I drove her men back to this boat. I then immediately turned around went back and picked her up. She thanked me for the ride back and was very gracious for the teasing I had given to her commissioned officer status.

One summer morning as the bars were letting out, the streets were rather crowded with people finding their way home. I looked to my right as I drove down one particular street that has most of the bars of the city on it. There, in a doorway to a closed business, I saw a man urinating against the doorjamb. I find this activity particularly disgusting and offensive. I shined my light on the gentleman, illuminating his frantic attempts to adjust his pants and hide himself. I noted that he was exceptionally intoxicated, and I approached him explaining that he would be locked up until he sobered up. He begged me not to do this. He explained that he was on leave from the Army, and if he did not make it back in time, he would be A.W.O.L. Still angry, I demanded his military ID and took note that he was a private. Pulling out my wallet, I displayed my military ID and my rank as a Staff Sergeant. The young drunken private immediately assumed the position of parade rest and again begged me not to lock him up. I looked him over and asked what his MOS was. He said that he was an 11 Bravo (infantryman). I explained to him that I was also an 11 Bravo, and if he gave me 50 push-ups, I would let his friends take him home rather than lock him up. He looked at me and smiled, and immediately dropped and began doing push-ups. I let him complete about four or five before I said, "I haven't heard one yet."

He immediately started counting, "One Sergeant, Two Sergeant, Three Sergeant, Four Sergeant." He completed the 50 push-ups, requested permission to recover, and once I told him he could recover, he jumped to his feet and walked off with his friends, thanking me profusely.

One morning at approximately 1 A.M., or about one hour before the bars close, I was checking the parking lot of a rather large club. I saw three men leave the club and jump up one at a time on a car near the entrance. They then ran across the hoods and trunks of several cars until they saw me and jumped down. I noted at this point that all three of these men were sailors, that is to say, a serviceman from the United States Navy. I saw that all three men were in their work utility uniforms. I happen to know that it is against regulations to leave the base or be out in public in that uniform. I'm also quite sure that there are several regulations about being drunk in public, causing disturbances etc. in uniform. I stopped all three men and demanded their identifications. They provided them and immediately began to beg that they not be locked up. They explained that their ship was due to sail the following day, and if they were locked up, they would miss that movement which would be a tremendous violation. As I walked and inspected all the cars, looking for damage, I asked them their names, the name of the ship they were assigned to, the Social Security numbers, and their ranks.

Seeing no damage to the cars, I tested each of the men for sobriety. Thankfully, one of them had been designated to stay sober, and I allowed him to drive his friends back to the ship. I then went to the station and accessed my military email account. After a little research, I was able to locate these gentlemen, their ship, and more importantly their commanding officer. I sent an email to their commanding officer explaining my encounter with these gentlemen, their state of dress, their state of sobriety, and their actions. A short time later, I received an email from the commanding officer of that ship who apologized for his men's actions. He also explained that they would meet with military justice for their actions.

Put the Wet Stuff on the Hot Stuff

It is no secret that a 'friendly' rivalry exists between police officers and firefighters. It seems only natural because both professions appear to attract a particular type of person. We both, police and firefighter, tend to be assertive, aggressive, and rather self-assured individuals. This leads to a competitive situation in which both groups see the other as an opponent. It is not that either of us actually dislikes or mistrusts the other. It is simply a case of two big dogs growling at each other from opposite sides of the fence. This growling often takes the form of jokes and gibes, nicknames and stereotypes.

I am not above any of this. I often will complain out loud about firefighters and the public's adoration of them. I will gripe about these men and women receiving the same pay that I do while they sleep, play video games, and cook chili. While I understand that containing and ultimately extinguishing a house fire is a daunting task, I will often make jokes about how it seems a relatively simple one. Anyone who has ever gone camping, or received any survival training, knows that starting and maintaining a fire is the actual task. It is well known that if you do not feed and tend a campfire, it will soon go out on its own. These men in their big red trucks, however, given an unlimited supply of water are hailed as heroes for putting out a fire. I would like to say again that I witnessed these men and women do their job, and I personally want no part of it. In the end, however, isn't it just wetting down the hot stuff?

One night in late fall, I was dispatched to a call regarding a fire alarm in an apartment building. The call notes indicated that there was thick smoke. I arrived well ahead of the firefighters. This was due to my advantage of already being awake and dressed. This was the early morning hours, approximately 3 A.M, and the firefighters had to get out of bed and get dressed, before starting their big red truck and driving to the scene. For my own sense of completion, I will mention here that the apartment building was less than 300 yards from the fire station. I arrived on scene and made my way to the second floor where the smoke seemed to be coming from. As I followed the smoke to what appeared to be its source, I found an apartment that was being renovated. Part of the renovation was having the hardwood floors sanded. Whoever was doing the work had left the catch bag from the sander sitting in the center of the floor. The fine sawdust from the sander, coupled with the wax and treatment of the floor was the perfect recipe for spontaneous combustion. This bag contained at its center smoldering ember that was producing the billows of smoke.

I made my way through the building, waking up the residents and getting them outside to avoid any problems with smoke inhalation. Once I had the building clear, which took me approximately 15 to 20 minutes, I made my way back inside. I went to the sink in the kitchen of the apartment that was being renovated. There I filled a gallon jug with water and started to walk over to the smoking bag. It was at this point that the firefighters arrived on scene. They made their way into the apartment with the enthusiasm a group of marines might have storming a beach. The ranking firefighter on scene

29

chastised me for attempting to pour water on the situation. According to him, this would've aggravated the situation, causing far more smoke. I acknowledged that he and his men were far more experienced in these situations and I backed off. What they did next baffled me, but again, they are the experts.

One of the firefighters (using the tool that they have for opening doors and prying car hoods) smashed out a kitchen window. Another, using a large shovel, picked up the bag of dust and smoke and dumped it out the newly removed window. As I watch this happen, I marveled at the firefighters' propensity for damage. I am sure there is a reason for everything they do. However, I have noted that they do seem to love breaking things. Looking down to the side yard where the bag had been dumped I saw that as it hit the ground, it burst. The hot embers inside, now exposed to the air, burst into flame. It was unfortunate that it landed in a pile of dry leaves, which also burst into flame. It was even more unfortunate that those accumulated leaves where in the corner of a wooden fence which by the time the firefighters exited the house and made their way to the side yard was also beginning to burn. I am no expert, but I think the new smoke my gallon of water would have caused would have been less damaging than their solution. I guess I could chalk all this up to the fact that they had just woken up and were probably still a bit groggy.

One night, several years after the 'smoking bag' incident, I was dispatched to an intersection not far from the same apartment building. It was, in fact, less than half a block away. The dispatcher informed me that I was to go to this intersection to meet with the fire department and one of their ladder trucks. Dispatcher further noted that the fire department believed that they 'may have' hit something. I arrived on scene and immediately saw one of the streetlights leaning into the street at approximately a 45° angle. I further noted that a large toolbox that is usually attached to the rear of the ladder truck was sitting on the street. I stepped out of my cruiser and announced to the firefighters assembled around the truck:

"I have solved the mystery as to whether or not you have hit something. You did. It was that streetlight."

They did not seem amused at all with my quip. The ranking firefighter approached me, and I asked what had happened. He informed me that they were making their way to back up another piece of apparatus. That they had left the station with their coats, helmets, hoses, and axes. They had forgotten, however, the man who was supposed to be driving the back half of the ladder truck. So as this multi-ton vehicle travel two blocks from the station, it's back half-drifted to the side and took out the streetlight.

The firefighters were rather upset with me for two reasons. The first reason was that I absolutely refused to write the report in any other way except to tell the exact truth about what happened. The second and probably main reason they were upset was because I simply could not stop laughing.

Sometimes It Comes Around

When I was in high school, if you looked at me, you would never believe that I would someday be a police officer. I was 5'10", 130 pounds, and extremely timid. I chose to surround myself with a small group of friends who were far more assertive and intelligent than I. This left me with the role of quiet supporter to any plans or conversations. In most of my classes, there was another gentleman of similar stature to me. For the purposes of storytelling, I will call him Ed. I do not name anyone while writing this book for anonymity purposes.

'Ed' was kind of middle-of-the-road when it comes to the pecking order of high school. He was not one of the cool kids, and he was picked on from time to time. The strategy that he chose to alleviate this was to select someone more timid than he was to pick on; thus, deflecting some of the attention from him to me. This shifted him from being the one picked on to the team of people picking on me. I understand this now as an adult, however as a teenager and a young man I only thought of him as an asshole.

By the time I was a uniformed police officer, operating on my own, at least five years had passed since high school. I had not seen nor even thought of Ed in those years. At the time of our parting, I had seen him as an overconfident adversary and had always assumed that he would be far more successful than I. With the passing years and the knowledge acquired as to how the world works, and how people work within that world, I now know differently. I also know differently because one night during my first year on the job I ran into Ed.

I was dispatched to an alarm call at a rather popular Italian restaurant in the North end of the city. I was working the overnight shift at this point, and it had been, up until this point, a tranquil and peaceful night. It was summer time and rather warm out. I exited my cruiser and began to walk around the building, conducting a standard check for an alarm call. As I approached the back side of the building, I noticed a basement window open. Before I had the opportunity to call in my findings, I observed two large gallon bottles of wine come up from the open window. The hands holding the wine placed them on the pavement, and the man attached to those bottles began to climb out of the window. I walked over and stood to the side watching the man climb up. As his upper torso cleared the window, he looked up, and our eyes met. I cannot tell you how exceptionally excited and happy I was at that moment.

"Well, hello, Ed," I said as calmly and conversationally as I could.

I reached down and grabbed Ed by the scruff of his collar. By this time, I had grown into my frame. I was now approximately 200 pounds, and my time in the army, as well as the Academy, had given me a few muscles. I pulled him from the window and planted him on his feet in front of me. He was a little drunk and a little scared, so it took him a few moments to recognize who was standing in front of him. To his credit, once he did recognize me, he attempted to fall back into the societal roles we had each held in high school. He spoke to me in that condescending tone he had used in high school.

"So now you're a cop. Wow, who would've thought a little fag like you would become a cop."

He was a little intoxicated. It seems that since high school Ed had become quite the alcoholic. I suppose that should have been evident to me as he had broken into a successful business and chosen to steal only wine. I would like to admit at this time that my initial instinct was to take advantage of the situation. I was alone. I had not called for any assistance or even informed dispatch that I had observed a break. No one was coming, and here stood in front of me my high school tormentor. He was now a man in bad health, and about 40 pounds lighter than me. I was well trained and more than capable of doing him some harm. I had a momentary fantasy about releasing four years of frustration upon his head. It was a fleeting thing, and it passed. I simply turned him around and cuffed him up properly. I advised him of his rights and called the situation in to control. I transported him to booking and turned him over to the Booking Sergeant, while I wrote my report.

During the booking process, Ed attempted multiple times to engage me in conversation. You would think that given his current situation, he would try to curry my favor as he was facing multiple felony charges. Ed could not let go of the roles we had held in high school, however. He spent the half hour that it took me to book him berating and insulting me. He alleged that my sole purpose in arresting him was retaliation for my being a nerd in high school. I walked over to him as I prepared to bring him to a holding cell and explained to him that had retaliation been on my mind he certainly would not be walking to the cell under his own power. I explained to him that I had always felt that he was an idiot and an ass. I had noted during the booking process, and through the information that I obtained while researching him, that he had done

34

absolutely nothing since high school. He worked a series of part-time jobs, had no higher education, and had really changed in only one way. He was now far more of an alcoholic than he had been, and he now had lost his ability to intimidate me.

Come in Control

Throughout this, and probably any future writing, I will have many passionate, disparaging, mean, and downright disrespectful things to say about police dispatchers. This is born of frustration and should in no way indicate my true feelings towards a group of professional people who are locked in a windowless room for hours at a time. A group of individuals who must, through a phone line, speak to emotional, angry, and, often uneducated persons and quickly perceive the problem, understand the problem, and translate that into some form of language. I have done this job. I know it is hard. This information, however, has in no way lessened my frustration at the sometimes-unimaginable stupidity. I had a captain who used to say, "You pay peanuts, you get monkeys." Well, we must pay some form of stupid peanut because there have been some instances that have boggled my mind.

On my department, we have a policy where if a business or residence has an alarm, that alarm must be registered with the city. A running total of false alarms are kept within dispatch, and when that number reaches a certain amount within a year, a fine would be levied by the city. The result of this is that when an officer clears an alarm as 'false,' that officer should receive from dispatch the information as to whether or not the alarm is a registered alarm and how many false reports have been tallied. It should sound something like this:

Officer: Yes control that will be a 4591. (Code for a false alarm.)

Dispatcher: Affirmative unit. That will be the fourth of the year and registered.

One night, I heard the car for the area adjacent to mine receive a call for an alarm at a business. I was close by and volunteered to take the call. It took me only a few minutes to clear the alarm as false. The building was secure. There were few points of access and no fences to climb to see all parts of the building. The simple dialogue above did not happen. Instead, I got the following:

Me: Unit 14 to control, 4591.

Dispatch: Yeah, Unit 14, what are you clearing?

Me: The alarm that I just told you I would take.

Dispatch: Unit 14 we sent 11 to that.

Me: Yes control and I told you that I would take it for them. (Pause). So 4591.

Dispatch: Okay 10–4

Me: Yes control I need the count.

Dispatch: That will be fourth of the year (NNNregistered).

Me: Control I copy fourth of the year, but did you say 'unregistered' or 'and registered'?

Dispatch: (long pause) Standby, wait for one, stand by, I'm trying to look it up. My computer just froze.

Now, this seems reasonable, computers freeze, however, I was not asking for this dispatcher to look anything up. What I was asking was for her to repeat what she had just said. The delay between her saying the unintelligible 'NNNregistered,' and my asking for clarification was less than two seconds. Her inability to answer me was baffling. I could only draw a few speculations. First, the person I spoke to was so completely brain-dead that her short-term memory lasted less than two seconds. Second, that she spoke such horrendous English that even she did not understand what came out of her mouth. Lastly, most probably, and to be frank, most frightening, was that so little attention was paid to my activities out on the street, that she really didn't have an idea what was going on and was only casually paying attention to our conversation. I had to go to the station and look up the statistics for that business myself. It was easier than trying to continue the line of questioning I had started with Dispatch.

There have been many things that I have noticed about dispatchers that have angered, or at least annoyed me. One is the qualifying statements that they tend to use when communicating with us. I've spent much of my time since I was a teenager as a part of a team, be it military or in police work. It is my opinion that when you are part of the team, you win or lose as a part of that team and can blame no one person for failure. Dispatchers, or at least my dispatchers, have developed a habit of saying things like 'my call taker told me' or 'the information I was given.' These statements are meant to imply that it is not the speaker's fault for any missing or false information. I believe that the dispatcher should use the word 'we' a lot more often. It is my opinion that the people saying this would feel as though they were part of a combined effort, and therefore be more diligent.

I have also noted that the dispatchers have a series of very common excuses that they use, oft times without even thinking if it is applicable. One of their favorite excuses is the 'delay.' When keying the microphone, there is an approximate one-second delay before transmission starts. Very often, the first word transmitted by someone in a rush will be cut off by this 'delay.' This is a common enough occurrence that it tends to be the 'go to' excuse for a dispatcher missing a transmission. Now, I understand that I seem a little harsh here as I am making accusations with little or nothing to back up my statement. I offer the following exchange that I overheard, perhaps not as proof but at least as reliable evidence.

Medic: Medic three to control we are clear and available.

Dispatcher: Last calling medic, the delay cut you out, which medic is this?

Now, as I explained, the delay happens at the beginning of a transmission. If in fact the medic had been cut off by the delay, it would have been the word medic and not the word three that would have been cut off. If, the first word had been cut off, how would the dispatcher have known it was a medic calling? It could have been any unit whose call sign ended in three. The delay had nothing to do with it. The dispatcher was simply not paying attention. The dispatcher did not wish to admit that they were not paying attention and therefore blamed the mythical delay.

Very often the call-takers and dispatchers will abbreviate and edit down many of the notes of the call, I assume for brevity and efficiency. However, often times, the space and speed gained from this leaves the officer lacking in information. I remember one morning at about 7 A.M. I was dispatched to a house with the all too brief notes:

"Child refusing to go to school."

This is not an uncommon call, as in these modern times parents will often call the police rather than discipline their own children, for fear of the 'abuse' accusation. I responded to the house and met the woman who placed the call outside. She was a woman in her early 40s, dressed quite sharply and obviously on her way to work. She looked at me and questioned why I was alone. I thought little of this and explained to her that I often work alone and asked where the child was. She directed me to the top of the stairs first room on the left, and I made my way inside.

I walked into the bedroom and saw there an unkempt bed with a large lump in the middle. I shook the bed with my foot and sternly told the occupant to get up. At this point, the information missing from the initial notes of the call would have been beneficial. It seems that this 'child' was 17 years old. He was 6'5" tall and weighed well over 260 pounds. The 'school' that he was refusing to go to was a court mandated anger management class. It seems that this order came as a result of his injuring four police officers who were attempting to arrest him a few weeks earlier. In retrospect, this does clarify his mother's initial questioning of my being alone. Seeing the boy's size, I quickly thought to myself that I was in an awful lot of trouble should he decide to be aggressive. The only thing I could think to do was to bluff and continue with my assertive demeanor. I ordered him to get dressed, I ordered him out of the house. He seemed to think about this for a moment but decided that he was too tired to argue. He got dressed and left the house. His mother explained to me that she simply did not want him to be in the house alone while she was at work, as his behavior had caused significant amounts of property damage in the past.

I thought for a moment about attempting to force this young man to go to his class. I determined, however, that discretion was the better part of valor. I advised him to go to his class. I reminded him that failing to go to the class would likely result in a warrant for his arrest. I watched him walk away after he acknowledged what I advised him. I honestly don't know if he attended that class that day and I have luckily never encountered him since.

One day during a rather heavy snowfall, I was dispatched to an address to meet a complainant regarding a neighbor dispute. I arrived and spoke with a woman who was irate that a neighbor had parked his car in a spot that she had shoveled out earlier that day. I explained to this woman with all the empathy that I could muster that while her neighbor was an inconsiderate ass, he was unfortunately not a criminal, and there was nothing I could do to rectify the situation. In truth, I checked the car thoroughly, ensuring it was 'legally' parked, registered, safe, etc. Had I found any excuse to tow it away, I would have, because like I said before, 'inconsiderate ass.' I again explained to this woman what the situation was, apologized, and left. I cleared the call as 'assisted.'

A short time later, I was dispatched to the same address. The call notes this time were that there was a bomb threat. I was outraged. How dare this woman use 'bomb threat' to get attention to a situation that I had already explained was unwinnable. Bear in mind that this was the winter of 2001, as you can imagine 'bomb threat' carried a lot of weight. I returned to the house, pounded on the door, and I was yelling before she had the door completely open. I informed this woman that calling in a false bomb threat was a felony, and she could easily find herself in jail over a simple parking spot. I pointed, I gestured, I raised my voice, and I'm sure some spittle flew. She looked at me in fear, and I was quite proud that my spectacle was having its desired effect. She then denied calling in a bomb threat.

41

That was it! This woman had crossed the line. First, she was stupid, but now she was lying to me. I walked to her phone. I picked it up and I dialed 911. The dispatcher answered and I identified myself. I requested to speak to the person who had taken this last call, the dispatcher was put on the line. I demanded an audio playback. I was going to show this liar that a bomb threat was no joke and I informed the dispatcher of such.

"Well," the dispatcher said hesitantly, "see, she was tough to understand, and I don't know what she said."

I was never quite so happy to not be able to reach the dispatcher because, honestly, had she been within my grasp, I would have gone to jail. I took a deep breath and let my words come out as slow and measured as I possibly could.

"You mean to tell me that you had no idea what you were sending me to? And so you just guessed? And your first *best* guess was 'bomb threat'?" I hung up. I left the woman's apartment without another word. By the time I reached my cruiser, a private message was on the dispatch board from the station sergeant warning me not to go into dispatch. It seems everyone was afraid of what I was going to do. I learned sometime later that that particular dispatcher went home sick rather than face me.

Working in New England snow is often a factor during our calls. I remember one night on an ambulance run, the ambulance could not get near the building. The snow in the parking area was thigh deep. The side streets around the building had not been plowed. The ambulance had to stay on the main road about 100 meters from the door of the building. I called dispatch and requested assistance. They sent me a truckload of firefighters and a second officer. Between all of us, we were able to carry the patient, who was suffering a stroke, through the parking area and over a stonewall to the rig. It had been snowing steadily for hours, and the plows had basically given up on everything but the main roads. While carrying our patient, the dispatchers chose to call the officer whom they had sent to assist me.

"Unit 15, we need you to go to the area of Cedar and Sycamore streets. (Two minor streets, Sycamore being a one-way.) We have complaints of a lot of snow in that intersection."

I remember that other officer looking at me, and without uttering a syllable, conveying the message to me, 'You heard that too, right? They are out of their minds.' This particular officer is almost as sarcastic as I am, and he responded exactly how I believe I would have.

"Control, first I am still on the medic call that you sent me to, second without going there I can guarantee you that there is a lot of snow at that intersection. The entire city is covered in a lot of snow. If in fact, I were able to get to that intersection and see the snow there, what exactly would you have me do about it?"

The dispatchers, of course, had no response for this whatsoever, and we chose to ignore it and handle the situation that truly required our attention. Several hours later, while attempting to log off and go home, the dispatchers insisted that that officer give them a clearance code for the call involving the snow. The officer became irate, and I calmed him by telling him I would handle it for him. I logged into the call assigned myself as the primary officer and entered the code for an emotionally disturbed/delusional person. I added to the call notes that only a delusional person would have dispatched us to that call, and, therefore, it was an appropriate clearance. I was chastised and threatened with a suspension on that one. Even today, years later, I believe it was totally worth it.

The implementation of computers into the whole dispatch system has made things far easier than they were when I started this job. When I first worked for the department, I spent some time as a dispatcher, and at that point, we filled out small index cards and handed them to the dispatcher. They were men who knew the job so well that if you give them an address, they could tell you what sector car handled that area without even researching. I remember one dispatcher who could give you the cross streets on any address and never be off by more than a block. In many cases, actually, in most cases, he could even describe the house to you. Now we have computers that tell the dispatcher what unit to send once a call is entered. It has taken all the thinking out of the equation. Because the thinking has been taken out, it is my opinion that many of the people working in that room pay little to no attention to what's going on and simply do what the computer tells them to do.

I offer as an explanation a call I received one day. The dispatcher sent me to a particular intersection that was at the very northeast corner of the city. What I mean by this standing in the center of that intersection is that if you take one step either north or west, you would be in a different town. If you typed in the street names at that intersection to our computer, it would tell you to send the particular car I was working that day. The call notes with a blue Chevy was traveling north at that intersection and doing greater than 100 mph. Now, if you put any thought into this at all, you realize that by the time you finish reading that sentence, the car has traveled quite a distance out of the city. Thinking, however, is no longer necessary because the computer tells you what to do. So I was dispatched to an intersection to look for a car that by the time I was made aware of it had traveled many miles away.

Often times, the dispatcher will need an officer to call them. It may be that the notes of the call are lengthy and need explanation. It may be that the nature of the call is of a sensitive nature and should not be put out over the air. Regardless of the reason, someone will call the unit on the radio and tell them to '21.' (The code for calling the station is 4521.) In the days before cell phones, the officer would have to find a pay phone, or an open business to make that call. These days with cell phones the call can be done instantly. In both instances what I found most frustrating was that after being told to '21' I would place that call and have to endure the following exchange:

Dispatcher: Communications how can I help you.

Me: Yes this is unit 15.

Dispatcher: Okay, what do you want?

Me: Someone just told me to call up there. Are you not in the same room as the person who asked me to call? Are you paying so little attention to what's going on that the person seated right next to you is speaking, and you're not hearing?

Police officers are not immune to poor communication, and the laziness inherent in the computer system. Since the computers have become a part of our daily lives, officers have begun to rely on them heavily. I constantly hear officers requesting the cross streets on addresses that they should know. They should at the very least be able to get to the general area and find it from there. It seems that now that there is a computer screen offices are demanding more and more information and often times do not think before asking the same questions at every call. I recall one night an officer being sent on a disturbance call. The notes of the disturbance call were that a naked man was disturbing in a particular intersection. I remember the officer asking for a description of the man. I know that he could not have thought that question through. The dispatcher's response to that question was perfect:

"Well, unit, when you get to that intersection, if you see two naked men we will try to get a description to narrow it down. Until then, however, I would just go with the naked guy as that is probably the one you're looking for."

Mommy

For the first five or six years of my career, bail was conducted at the police station. We had our own holding cells, and a clerk of courts would come in every three hours. Most often he would release people on their own recognizance, charging them a fee to do the paperwork. During the time that this story takes place, the fee was $25. On occasion, the clerk will assign cash bail in addition to the fee, and that money would be returned to the defendant when he or she arrived at court.

One particularly cold and snowy winter night, I was assigned as the booking officer. It was my job to maintain the books and log in and out of each prisoner. I was also to assist with the booking of any prisoners and help the desk officer in any way he needed. Like I said, this was a frigid and very snowy night, and I was somewhat glad to have inside duty. Around 3 A.M. the clerk of courts came in to conduct the bail. A couple of men bailed themselves out, and the clerk was preparing to leave when a woman walked in the front doors. She shook off a massive amount of snow. Her face was flushed, and she was shivering. She looked to be in her early 60s, she stood about 5'2", and though difficult to tell through her heavy jacket, I don't think she could have weighed more than 110 pounds. I spoke with her and learned that she had come here to bail her son out. She had walked the better part

47

of 2 miles to get this done. She was very relieved that she had not missed the clerk.

I went downstairs, got her son out of the cell, and brought him upstairs to be processed out. He stood just under 6 feet. He was overweight, not fat; it was just apparent that he had never done any physical exercise or hard work. As the paperwork was being filled out, his mom asked quite a few questions. The questions didn't slow the clerk down; he was a professional and more than capable of doing both at once. The questions, however, were quite aggravating to her son; and at one point toward the end of the whole thing, he yelled at his mother.

"What the fuck, Ma, just sign the fucking paper so we can go, quit asking so many fucking questions."

I could see the hurt in the woman's eyes. I suppressed my urge to punch her son several times. She looked at the clerk with tears in her eyes and asked, "Do I have to bail him out?"

"You absolutely do not have to," responded the clerk as he crumpled up the paperwork and returned her money to her. She turned to walk out the door and her son cried out, "Mommy, wait!"

I was not going to let this young man manipulate this woman after he had just hurt and humiliated her. I grabbed him by the wrist and elbow and escorted him quickly down to the cells. I will admit that he did not go gently into the cell, but I didn't injure him either.

I raced back upstairs and begged the woman to stop for a moment and sit down. I brought her some tissue and a cup of water to help her settle down and asked her politely to wait. I then went to the patrol lieutenant's office and asked his permission to call in a cruiser to give this woman a ride home. After explaining the entire series of events to the lieutenant, he granted permission. A cruiser was called in, and as luck would have it, they were the men who had arrested her son in the first place. Once the situation was explained to them, they were more than happy to give this woman a ride back to her home.

Ewwwww!

Police work is a lot of things; dull, exciting, scary, frantic, and sometimes gross. There have been numerous instances throughout my career where I struggled to keep my lunch down. The sights and smells the police officer is subjected to would often send a sane man running. Dead bodies, trash, and insects, and a surprising amount of feces are just part of the day-to-day encounters an officer contends with.

I recall one of the local drunks, we will call him Harold. Harold was a tall, large black man in his mid-30s. Harold spent a great deal of his time homeless and even more of his time intoxicated. Thinking back, I'm 100% certain that I never saw Harold sober. This lifestyle did not leave Harold with a lot of time for grooming or bathing. Being close to Harold, say within 5 feet, subjected someone to a foul stench that is beyond literary description. In addition to the odor, there were a number of times that Harold was infested with bugs of one type or another. I have a clear recollection of assisting medical personnel in loading Harold onto an ambulance. While lifting up the stretcher and looking Harold in the face, I clearly saw a bug. I'm no expert, but I believe it was some form of lice. While lifting the stretcher, I watch this bug crawl out of the tangle that was Harold's beard, move across his face, and crawl into his nose. I was about to mark that in my memory as one of the most utterly disgusting sites I had ever seen when I observed dozens of other similar bugs moving throughout his hair and beard and crawling in and out of his nose and ears. I don't know how I maintained my cool, or my lunch but I loaded Harold onto the ambulance and sent him to the hospital. It is beyond my understanding how, but Harold is still alive 25 years later, and, I am sad to say, no cleaner and no less intoxicated.

Bugs are not innately gross, at least not to me. I have spent hours fascinated by a spider spinning its web, or watching a beetle chew its way through a leaf. Great masses of bugs, however, I find downright unnerving. One morning while answering a call in an unusually small and rundown apartment, I stood by as other officers conducted interviews. While standing by I looked around the room as I have learned that it is always best to remain alert and inquisitive. My eye was drawn to some movement on the top of the stove. I shone my light over the top of the stove and was utterly repulsed. The top of the small gas stove had what I estimate to be a quarter inch of old, built-up grease. The food that remained in the frying pan sitting atop the burner was to my best guess, two days old. The movement that had caught my eye was dozens, if not hundreds of roaches. They were moving about the top of the stove, giving it the appearance of a single swirling mass. I tapped my fellow officer on the shoulder and pointed the situation out to him. He finished up his interview with incredible speed, and we left the building at almost a dead run. When we got outside into the street, I saw my partner jumping up and down and stamping his feet with ferocity in the street. I watch this for a few moments with what must have been a rather quizzical look on my face. He turned to me and explained himself.

"I feel like the bugs are crawling all over me, I need to shake them off."

There is something about the smell of the decomposing human body that is unique in the world. I remember before I got on the job, reading a story about the investigation into a serial killer. I remember the investigating officers stating that in speaking with the suspect they could smell in the house 'the smell of death.' This was due to several bodies being buried in the crawlspace beneath the house. I remember at the time, having no frame of reference, how those officers were able to identify that smell, in such a passing encounter. Having since then encountered that smell on several occasions, I now know that I too would be able to identify it the moment I detected it.

During my time in detectives, I had to respond to the scene of many deaths. It was our responsibility to investigate any unattended death, until such time as foul play could be ruled out. On one such call out, I had with me a junior detective as it was my job to show him the ropes. We arrived at an apartment building that was one of the larger buildings in the city. It is five stories high with an all brick exterior and encompassed two-thirds of the city block. The apartment we were headed to was on the third floor. As we walked into the lobby, I immediately detected the faint smell of a human body decomposing. I turned to the young man who was with me and told him to prepare himself. He asked why, and I looked at him stunned. I asked him if he had ever encountered a 'stinker' before. After I had explained that a stinker was slang for the decomposing body, he confessed that he had not yet encountered one. As we made our way up the stairwell, the odor became stronger and stronger. When we opened the apartment door, which until that moment had been guarded by a patrolman, the smell absolutely overwhelmed us. Seeing detectives arrive on the scene, the patrolman who had been standing guard exited the building with all due haste. My young charge and I entered the apartment and began to look around.

We found the deceased man, in his underwear lying partially in and partially out of the bathtub. His skin was mottled and had a slight sheen to it. I recognize this as an indicator that he had been decomposing for the better part of a week. The smell within that enclosed and the small apartment was overwhelming. I was dealing with it fairly well as I had encountered it before. My young protégé was not doing well at all. After looking over the scene and taking notes, we called for the appropriate persons from the Medical Examiner's Office and set about waiting for the body to be removed. By this time, I'm sure my young partner was questioning his decision to transfer to the detective division. He had opened a window and was sticking his head and most of his upper torso out of the building in an attempt to breathe air that was not fouled. Every so often I would stick my head out the nearby window to speak with him and tell him about observations I had made within the apartment so that we could keep comparable notes.

When the workers from the Medical Examiner's Office arrived, I told my protégé to prepare himself because "things are about to get worse."

"Oh my God! It gets worse!?" he exclaimed incredulously.

I will never forget the look of absolute horror on his face as he asked me this. I saw fear. I saw disbelief. I saw the look in his eye that begged me to say it wasn't so. I explained to him that it was, in fact, going to get much, much worse. You see, when a body is decomposing in this way, fluids are

53

building up along with gases inside the body that have not yet found an escape route. When the body gets moved, these fluids and gases will find their way out of a variety of orifices. This is known in some circles as 'purging.' I wasn't lying and when the body was moved the purging commenced. This was one of the foulest examples that I can recall. Even the workers from the Medical Examiner's Office were taken aback. I had to step outside to regain my composure. My young partner was leaning so far out of the window that I genuinely feared he was going to fall.

There is a woman in my city that at one time was on stage for the Miss America pageant. She was the representative of our state and an absolutely stunningly beautiful woman. Within seven years of that pageant, she had become a heroin user/addict. The failing health, track marks, and lack of hygiene made it actually difficult for a casual observer to see the beautiful woman that had once been there. I remember a conversation with her as I looked over the bruised and infected track marks up and down each of her arms. I remember asking her what she was going to do as it looked like she was going to soon run out of places to inject herself. This once beautiful woman opened her mouth full of rotted and broken teeth, lifted her tongue, and displayed fresh track marks inside and under her tongue.

I could probably fill several books with some of the disgusting sights and smells I have encountered. Autopsies, car accidents, dead infants, and a variety of wounds that have shown me the insides of bodies that people were just not meant to see. That is not the mood that I wanted this book to inspire. So let's move on to happier thoughts.

At Least the Bugs Are Gone

One morning as I was finishing up reports, I heard a call over the radio indicating that there had been an explosion in an apartment building. This particular apartment building is 10 floors and contains hundreds of apartments. The residents of this building are almost exclusively the elderly, and those with disabilities. That particular morning there was a lack of available units, and I volunteered to jump in with the street Sgt. who was rushing to the scene. When we arrived, we were directed by the firefighters to the seventh floor.

When we first arrived, I noted that there were several residents in the hallway being directed either back to their apartments or out of the building. I also observed that the doors to the apartments in this building all opened into the apartment. Apartment number 721, however, had a door that now opened out. I was introduced to the resident of that apartment. He was an elderly man in his early 70s. He explained to me that he had a large bug problem in his apartment and had set off several bug bombs to take care of the situation. He stated that as he was leaving the apartment, he heard a loud boom and was blown across the hall into the wall. Despite my best efforts, I could not convince this man to seek medical attention, he insisted that he was fine. I try to explain that even though he didn't feel any ill effects right now, it really was unknown what if any damage had been done. Several neighbors as well as

55

building management explained that this gentleman was experiencing Alzheimer's and that the bugs he was combating were purely imaginary.

Once the scene was cleared by firefighters, I made my way inside to investigate. Inside, I found the bug bombs that had been set out. Upon reading the packaging, I noted that the gentleman had used at least three times the amount recommended for an apartment his size. I also learned that the propellant used in this type of pest elimination system is a form of propane. Instructions on the box indicated that all pilot lights in the area should be extinguished before the devices are used. I also noted that all the windows in the apartment had been sealed shut with several layers of duct tape. The resident explained that he did this to keep the bugs out. It had the effect of keeping the gas contained. When the bug spray and its propellant reached a significant concentration and rose to the level of the pilot lights on the stove, there was ignition and explosion.

The force of the explosion had pushed the inward opening door out and knocked the resident across the hall. The explosion had also raised the ceiling in the living room about 1 inch off the walls. The force of the blast had also pushed the adjoining wall to apartment number 723 into apartment 723. In speaking with the resident there, an elderly woman, she explained what she experienced. She was sitting on her sofa, working on a jigsaw puzzle and watching television. The television was against the wall adjoining number 721. She heard the explosion and then suddenly the television, its stand, and the wall itself came rushing toward her. In a panic, she ran from the apartment. While inspecting her apartment, I noted a walker by the door. I asked this short plump and very nervous woman how she had managed to run from the apartment without her walker. She explained that fear was a great motivator. I accepted this at face value because fear has been a great motivator for me many times.

Over the next few days, I worked with the management of the building to contact the gentleman who had set off the bug bombs and his family. It was decided that given his degrading mental status and the potential for self-injury that he would be sent to a facility where he could be cared for. It is strange to think that this man's delusions of ants crawling around his apartment could've easily cost hundreds of lives. Everyone was fortunate that day that the resulting explosion had not done more damage and had not threatened the structural integrity of the building.

The apartment, actually the apartments were repaired. I have been back to both of those apartments several times over the years. I've usually been there for medical calls. There have been many subsequent residents. Each time I go to those apartments, I can still see the cracks and repair work and I feel compelled to retell the story to anyone who will listen.

My Wife the Hero

I have been truly blessed. My wife is my perfect partner. She enjoys almost all of the odd things that I like. We are obsessed with almost all of the same television shows. She likes the same video games I do. She enjoys spending time with my friends. I love my wife, not because of these things, but I honestly love every bit of her. I'm truly appreciative of how lucky I am. I was already a police officer for a long time when I met my wife. She has, over the years, been learning to be an officer's wife. She is doing very well, and I believe at this point she could actually give a seminar to young women contemplating a life with the police officer.

She has learned to live with the odd and unpredictable hours. She has learned to deal with her husband getting a phone call and jumping into his uniform to go and work an overtime shift. She knows that when out at a restaurant I need to sit with my back to the wall. She knows that for a view the door is essential as I want to see who is coming and going. She is patient with me when I walk into a new place and pause to scan the entire area. She deals with the fact that I will randomly slow down while driving through the city to observe something that seems out of place to me. She deals with the fact that I will stop and check with every officer I see, either working the detail or out of the traffic stop, to ensure that they are okay, and ask if they need anything. She has even developed the habit of keeping some water in the car to offer to officers who are working a road job on hot summer days.

One evening, while returning home from a night out, we observed a car moving along the highway and weaving horribly. This newer model, the four-door luxury car had gone into the breakdown lane no less than three times in under 2 miles. It also weaved over from the right lane to the center lane a couple of times. My immediate estimation was that it was a drunk driver. I took out my cell phone, dialed the number for the state police, placed it on speaker, and handed it to my wife so that she could hold it up to my head. She did all of this without complaint, as a matter of fact, there was some enthusiasm for helping me. Once I had the state police dispatcher on the line, I gave out a description of the car, our location, as well as the direction of travel, and volunteered to stay on the line to keep the dispatcher updated.

In short order, the state police cruiser caught up with us. I informed the dispatcher that I had sight of the cruiser and put my arm out the window to give that officer a thumbs-up signal. I ended the call with the dispatcher and slowed down to give the cruiser ample space to get between me and the suspect vehicle. I turned to my right to look at my wife as we pulled over into the breakdown lane about 50 yards behind where the trooper had conducted his traffic stop. She had pulled out a notebook and a pen and had begun making notes as to our observations. My amazing wife was acting more conscientiously than most of the rookies I work with, and I told her as much. We waited while the trooper conducted a traffic stop so that should he need our names as witnesses we would be available to give statements. After a few minutes, the trooper allowed the other car to drive off and walked back to speak to us. We were rather shocked as I could not figure any way that the driver was not completely intoxicated. The weaving and random acceleration and deceleration looked like a training video for detecting drunk drivers.

The trooper came over and introduced himself to us, and we to him. I explained to him again our observations, and he smiled. He looked into the car, and after seeing my wife, he paused. I could see he was doing some mental editing to tell the story that he wanted to tell in front of a woman. He then told us what had happened.

The trooper explained that the driver was not alone in the car as I had reported. We had observed the car quite carefully, and my wife and I had both agreed that all we could see was an operator. The trooper explained that there was a reason we couldn't see the passenger. It seems that the female passenger was not sitting upright in the car. The female passenger was lying across the driver's lap and was "being very nice to him." This was the euphemism that the trooper had chosen to explain the situation in front of my wife, a woman whose delicacies he was unaware of. My wife while being a polite, educated, and well-spoken young lady, is also well aware of the world, and the happenings therein. She is also not afraid to speak her mind.

"So she was blowing him," my wife interpreted out loud for the trooper.

He laughed a little nervously, and we parted ways.

One warm Saturday night in early fall, my wife and I were out with friends out of town. We had not seen these friends in quite some time, and my wife opted to stay while I went home to go to work. I got to work at midnight and proceeded to go from call to call for the next several hours. It was so hectic that it was difficult to get any 'air time' on the radio at all.

Sometime, just after 2 A.M., my wife called my cell phone. I answered, thinking that she was just telling me that she was home safe and to wish me a safe shift. She informed me however that she could hear noises in the house next door. We knew that the house was empty and up for sale, and there certainly should have been no persons inside at that hour. I asked her if she had called dispatch to report this, and she told me that she had. She said that that had been about ten minutes prior and that she was getting very nervous.

As I said it was a hectic night, and getting any air time whatsoever was difficult. I had just been clearing a disturbance call, and there were other offices with me. However, I was not going to raise them on the radio. So I decided to activate my blue lights and start heading to my home, thinking that the other offices would see the lights and follow out of curiosity. I was right, and two other officers followed along. We arrived, and as I exited my car, I explained to those who followed the situation. Looking over the house, I immediately found a basement window broken in. I transmitted into the near constant chatter that the busy night was producing and got dispatches attention. I informed them that I had a break in progress and gave them the address requesting additional units and a Clear Channel.

To explain, the Clear Channel is when all radio traffic in the city is relegated to one channel, and the other channel is left exclusively for the units handling a particular situation, like a break in progress. Dispatch informed me that they had 'just' received a call for a 'loud party' at that address. Now, I knew two things: one, my wife had made that call over ten minutes prior, and two, my wife is not an idiot and is more than

61

capable of explaining the difference between a burglar and a party. I informed dispatch that I really didn't care what their call notes said, I was dealing with a break in progress, and that's how I needed it handled. Despite dispatches' efforts to hinder me, several officers arrived on scene unprompted, having heard my plea.

I then went to the small basement window and determined that I was not going to get inside with my duty belt on. I was not as skinny as I had been when I started the job and the window was small. Unhooking my duty belt, I handed it to an officer close by and went into the basement headfirst. The landing was less than graceful. I would like to tell you that I slithered through the window like a viper hunting its prey. I would like to claim that I did a perfect shoulder roll and came to my feet ready for whatever threat I might face. I would like to claim all these things, but in reality, I tore my shirt on the glass and belly flopped to the basement floor, knocking the wind out of me and destroying a plastic lawn chair. Gaining my feet, I began to search the basement and noted that many of the copper pipes were broken. This is not an uncommon thing for thieves. They will often break into empty buildings to steal copper and sell it as scrap. As I scanned the room and looked up to the window that I had crawled through, I noted several faces of other offices peering down at me. At this point, I also noticed that I was the oldest man on scene by at least 12 years. I determined at that point to change how I did things.

Continuing to scan the basement, I found the culprit standing crouched, facing the corner with his hands covering his face. This was the same way a child might hide his face to count before hide and seek. I can only guess that he was hoping that if he couldn't see me, I couldn't see him. I grabbed him by the scruff of the neck, tossed him to the ground, and proceeded to handcuff him. I found my way out of the house, threw the burglar to a fellow officer while I went to check on my wife. As I walked up to my driveway, I saw my beautiful wife peeking out the side door, and she timidly asked, "Was it something?" She informed me that she had heard the banging in the basement and had initially thought an animal, perhaps a raccoon, had gotten in. She then observed a light, like a flashlight, moving around in the cellar, and knowing that raccoons almost never use flashlights, she decided to call it in. This was the information that my 'brilliant' dispatches had interpreted as a 'loud party.'

Upon searching my suspect, I found several items on his person, several of which I kind of expected to find. There were pliers and a screwdriver, standard instruments for a burglar. In addition, I found a flashlight on his person, and in the basement, a large canvas bag partially stuffed with broken bits of copper pipe. Most interesting was an item found in his back pocket. There I located one of those magazines that real estate agents put out with all the local houses for sale. He had circled in red ink the ad for the house we found him in, along with several others in the immediate area. Thankfully, upon inspection, we found none of the other homes broken into. It seems that my wife's quick thinking stopped what could have been a rather impressive crime spree.

Despite all the information that showed this man was prepared to do untold damage to multiple properties for a small sum of cash, he was offered a deal by the district attorney's office and spent only 18 months in county lockup. It is often said that 'the wheels of justice grind slowly.' I'm here to tell you that they also wobble and tend to weave randomly and without direction.

Of particular note, exactly 18 months later, and less than five houses away, I caught the very same man doing the very same thing. This time, however, he had broken the water pipe before the shut-off valve. This meant that as the basement flooded, we had no way to shut the water off and had to call the city to shut it off at the street. The burglar was again found in the basement. He again had flashlight pliers and a screwdriver. He again had a canvas bag (I actually think it was the same one) and he again had done thousands of dollars' worth of damage. He did a slightly better job of hiding as we found him behind the oil tank, covered in dirt, grease, and cobwebs.

This time while doing the paperwork, and frustrated with his consistency, I did some research on the history, 'criminal' history, of this gentleman. I found that he had been convicted of breaking and entering, burglary, and other related crimes a significant number of times within a short span of years. This information allowed me working with the district attorney's office to charge him as a 'career criminal.' That carried a sentence of 10+ years in state prison. This was a rare instance where the good guys won.

Off to Work We Go and Home Again

There is an expression that has been vocalized a dozen different ways, that essentially says, 'a police officer is always on duty.' Most police officers shrug at this and will at times emphasize their reluctance to do something off-duty. In my heart, I believe that no officer on or off-duty would ever let an emergency or life-threatening situation go on in their presence without acting in some manner. I have been lucky in that the situations which called for my action off-duty have almost always required nothing more than my being a genuinely good witness. I have called in suspicious persons and stood by observing until police arrived and then directed the arriving officers. I have called in and followed suspected drunken drivers until a marked unit could pull them over. I have broken up fights and rendered first aid at accidents. There have been, however a few occasions where I believe my off-duty activities were of note.

One day, at the end of my shift, I was driving home. The streets in my neighborhood are rather tight and mostly one-way. On this particular rainy fall morning, the road I was traveling on was blocked by an ambulance. Rather than backup three-quarters of a block to go around, and seeing no cruiser nearby to assist the ambulance I pulled over and got out to assist. I located the house where the medics were working on a patient. Upon entering, I immediately noted that the older building had rather small rooms and tight hallways. I anticipated that the medics would have some difficulty negotiating a stretcher out of the building. I began moving furniture and other items to create a path so that they might quickly make their way to their rig. The medics thanked me for my assistance, and once they had driven away, I went home to my wife. Once home and completely exhausted from the previous shift, I stripped off my uniform and crawled into bed.

A short time later, my wife woke me up, telling me that the station was on the phone and needed to speak to me. I wiped the sleep out of my eyes and checked the clock. I had only been asleep for about an hour. The officer who was on the phone asked me if I had assisted medics earlier that day on my way home, and I replied that I had. The officer then informed me that I had to report to the hospital. It seems the patient that the medics had transported had died shortly after arriving at the hospital. The concern was that he was suffering from meningitis. I had to report to the hospital to be checked out, and at the hospital, I was given an enormous pill to swallow as a precautionary measure. At the hospital, I was informed that since I was not on duty when it happened, dispatch had no idea who the officer was when the medics told them that that officer needed to be checked out. The medics had to come into the station and go through the department personnel file photos until they located me. In the end, I did not contract meningitis, and being that I had no physical contact with the patient, I was never in any real danger. Truth be told, I never got within 10 feet of them. I was just there to move furniture.

I have been fortunate in that I have always lived very close to where I was to report to work. I have never been more than

66

5 miles from the station I worked from, and for at least a quarter of my career, I've worked approximately three-quarters of a mile from my station. This lucky situation combined with the fact that parking around my station is rather involved has prompted me to walk to work quite often. I have been advised against this as my superiors think that my walking in uniform could make me a target, but to them, I say, I walk around that very area outside of my cruiser all the time. Their counterargument to this is that at least when I'm working, dispatch knows where I am. I've always shrugged this off, saying that being looked over by our dispatchers does not fill me with confidence in the first place.

One night, on 11 P.M., as I walked to work along a busy street, my attention was drawn to the sound of running water. As I rounded a corner, I saw a man standing at the edge of the sidewalk urinating in the street. He was an older man probably in his mid-50s. He was dressed rather shabbily, and his hair was wiry and unkempt. Beyond the fact that he was urinating in the street, he displayed all the outward signs of being intoxicated. I stood back and waited for him to finish. I have learned that it is best not to call out to someone engaged in this activity as they will inevitably turn towards the sound of your voice. This has the rather nasty side effect of aiming a stream of urine toward you. Once the man finished, I noted two women driving by in a car whose faces told me that they were shocked and disgusted by what they saw. I quietly walked up to the man as he put his equipment away and arrested him on the spot. At this point, I realized that I was only two blocks from the station. Walking him into the station was far easier than calling it in and waiting for a cruiser. I grabbed his elbow and walked him the two blocks to the station. Once there, I contacted station Sgt. who assisted me in cuffing the gentleman to a bench just inside the station. I went inside, attended roll call, signed out my car, and then took my prisoner to booking.

On the main road that leads from my city to the next town east, there is a river which constitutes the border between the two cities. In that river, there is an island which is the last part of my city before the town. On that island are several businesses to include a nightclub. I have been to that club on multiple occasions while on duty as it is within my patrol area and has been a rather busy club. I have often assisted at closing time in moving the crowds along. This activity has led me to somewhat befriend the staff there as we have worked in tandem moving the crowds along on numerous occasions. One evening, while off-duty, I was driving home past this club when I noted one of the security men standing in the parking lot arguing with another man. Security man was a slightly overweight gentleman who took his job very seriously. Some might say he's a little overzealous, but at least he tries to do a good job. As I stepped out of my car to make sure that he was all right, I noted that the man he was arguing with seemed to be first very young, perhaps even a teenager, and also exceptionally drunk. He was dressed rather nicely in shirt and tie with khaki pants and dress shoes. He had on a heavy leather jacket, which made sense as it was an icy winter night. As I approached, I asked the security man what the situation was.

He explained to me that the man he was arguing with had been at the club earlier that night celebrating his 21st birthday. He explained further, that the celebration had gone a little too far and that the club management and determined that it was in everyone's best interest that this man take a taxi home. The club had paid for the taxi and sent the man on his way. Forty-

68

five minutes later, this man arrived back with the intentions of driving his car away. The security officer was attempting to stop him. While I was receiving this explanation, the young man in question was becoming more and more agitated. I instructed him to calm down; I further explained to him that if he attempted to drive his car, I would, in fact, be placing him under arrest. As I made this last statement, I displayed my badge and identification. At this point, the drunken young man removed his leather coat threw it to the ground and shouted, "Fuck you, chase me!"

He then took off running toward an area of the island where boats are stored for the winter. My security friend began to give chase, but I stopped him by grabbing his shoulder and asked, "Why chase him? We are on an island. Where is he going to go?"

I pulled out my cell phone and called communications and explained to them the situation. Within a few minutes, I had a few cruises there to assist in the security officer and I gave him statements. As the car was within a private lot, we requested that the club have it towed away. They filled out the proper paperwork, and the car was soon towed away. In the meantime, the search of the island commenced. Initially, officers were unable to locate the gentleman in question. One by one the officers were called away to other calls, and we had to assume that the gentleman had somehow snuck off the island without us observing. Several hours later, as dawn approached, workers at the boatyard reported hearing the man calling for help. He was found in the boat yard hiding under some scaffolding. It seems that in hiding from us while lying on the ground and remaining perfectly still, he had felt the need to relieve himself. Not wanting to give up his position to the searching officers he'd simply urinated in place. The subzero temperatures of that evening cause the urine to freeze, thus freezing our would-be escapee, to the ground. He was arrested for trespassing and brought to the hospital for hypothermia. He really should've appreciated the free cab ride more.

I Can't Get No

The very first time I took a vacation by myself after graduating the police Academy, I went to Las Vegas for a few days. I was about three years on the job and I decided that I would enjoy myself. I remember going through brochures while sitting in a coffee shop, and planning my trip. The waitress at the coffee shop was a very old friend of mine and a very staunch Christian. I don't judge anyone for their faith or beliefs; I simply ask the same of them. I will not indicate where my beliefs lie as I do not believe this book is the proper venue for that discussion. Suffice to say that I am not a zealot to any belief system. While I was perusing the brochures, my friend stopped by to refill my coffee. Seeing the advertisements, she informed me:

"Las Vegas? You know that's the city of sin."

I think very highly of this woman, and again judge no one by their belief systems. Because I judge no one that means no one escapes my sarcasm.

"Oh my, I hope so. If it turns into the city of poetry reading before I get there, I will be wholly disappointed."

I selected a hotel to stay at and booked a flight, and my vacation was underway. I arrived in Las Vegas shortly after midnight and checked into my hotel as soon as I hit the city. I took a brief nap and awoke early to take a walk and see some sights. It was early morning in Vegas (before 8 A.M.), and the strip was relatively quiet. As I walked past Caesars casino, a flash of movement caught my eye up ahead of me. I saw a young man who was dressed in clothing that had not been washed, in my estimation ever. His appearance led me to believe that he had not bathed at least since he bought the clothing. He was a white man with long stringy blond hair, and he made a quick move and dashed at an elderly woman walking ahead of him. This put the woman between him and me at a distance of about 20 yards. He ran past her, grabbing her purse as he ran yanking it from her grip and knocking her to the ground. I ran forward and met him as we were both at a dead sprint in opposite directions. I drove my shoulder into him and knocked him clean off his feet. I very quickly pinned his arms behind him and held him to the ground hoping that help would arrive.

Help did come in very short order. It took the form of two young Las Vegas Metro police officers on bicycles. It seems that they had observed the entire thing happen from some distance away. They very quickly gathered me, the victim, and the bad guy up and ushered us into an alley between some casinos. As they were giving me the standard speech about civilians becoming involved in police work, I was able to identify myself, and their attitude changed. They very quickly explained to me that the reason for the quick trip to the alley is that the department tries very hard to keep all police activity out of sight of the general populace. Las Vegas makes its money off of tourism, and there is no sense in scaring the tourists. I was contacted by the local district attorney's office sometime later to ask if I would be willing to come out and testify. This would have been a windfall for me as I would have been paid by the department to go and give the testimony, and my accommodations would have been paid for by the district attorney's office. It turns out that the young man pled guilty in court, and I never had to go back out.

One night while off-duty, I went one state over to try my hand at night clubbing. I was not very successful; my personality is not one that thrives in that environment. After some failed efforts, by that I mean hitting on and being rejected by women, I was walking past some smaller clubs, looking for the parking area where I had left my car. I heard a shout behind me.

"Police, don't move!"

I turned to look, thinking this would be exciting. As I wondered what could possibly be going on, I saw three city police officers pointing their guns at me. I froze in place and knelt down. I crossed my legs behind me and placed my hands on top of my head interlacing my fingers. In a loud and clear manner, I stated:

"I am an off-duty police officer. I am unarmed. My badge and identification are in my right back pocket. I will not move unless instructed to do so."

The offices moved forward and cuffed me. They took out my badge and identification and confirmed what I said. They then informed me that there had been a stabbing at a club nearby. They told me that I fit the description of the suspect very well, down to the blue and white striped shirt that I was wearing. I informed them that I understood and would willingly return to the scene for a show-up identification.

At the scene, I was shown to two gentlemen and one rather intoxicated female. Both gentlemen agreed that I was not the suspect as I was several inches too short. The drunk woman said she wasn't sure. While this was going on, I looked over the scene and determined that the stabbing was a rather serious one. There was blood everywhere. It looked as if someone had filmed a 70s slasher movie in the club. I turned to one of the officers as he was uncuffing me and asked him to make note that with all the blood on the scene my body and clothing were free of any blood stain. He stated he would, collected my information, and sent me on my way. I never heard anything further from that incident.

My wife and I took a vacation to her hometown in eastern Virginia. We rented a house with the express purpose of doing absolutely nothing for a week. We visited with family, we ate at restaurants, but mostly, we rested; because to be honest, I needed the rest badly. One night about midway through our trip, my wife informed me that we were running low on toilet paper. I volunteered to walk to the store, which was about three blocks away, to get some. I didn't quite make it that far. About 60 yards from the driveway of the house we were renting, I heard a woman screaming for help. Looking up the first side street, I saw a young blond woman running into the street, screaming for help. I ran to her as quickly as I could and identified myself as an off-duty and out-of-town police officer. She told me that there was a man in her house whom she did not know. She pointed to a house with an open door. I handed her my cell phone and told her to call 911. I then entered the house and attempted to do a quick search. Before I could complete the search, she ran in behind me, thrusting the phone into my hands saying she could not make it work.

I called 911 and was quickly connected to the local police department. I gave all the pertinent information, including the address that I had to get from the hysterical woman. It was at this point that I realized that she was dressed only in a T-shirt and her panties. She must have been terrified to run out of the house in that state. She then informed me that the man had been in the bathroom, and I quickly search there. Finding no one, I moved on to the rest of the house and insured nor was there. The local PD came, and I gave them my statement and informed them that I had personally not seen the suspect. While waiting for the officers to clear the house and speak with the victim, I called my wife and let her know I would be a little late and why. A short time later, she walked up to meet me and watched me speak with the police officers.

"You just can't take a day off, can you?" my wife asked rather matter-of-factly. Then, we went to buy toilet paper.

How I Broke My Leg

I don't know if any of you have ever attempted to drive an older rear wheel drive car, like say a Ford Crown Victoria, under snowy or icy conditions. I can say that I do know, firsthand, what it's like to attempt this. I can also say that it is difficult (actually the words I have to say about driving a car in that manner don't belong in the book that might be picked up by children). Acceleration is non-existent, stopping almost always includes the slide in some random direction, and turning is something that needs to be planned, timed, and prayed upon. I have spent hours attempting a three-point turn or climbing the slightest incline for a block. It is no way for a person to respond to emergencies. Years ago, chains would be fixed to the tires of the cars so that some traction might be had. However, the damage caused by loose chains to the cars, or any chains to streets without snow; proved to be monetarily unwise.

When the Department began to purchase some SUVs, it became the practice to double, and sometimes triple up officers in these vehicles rather than risk their safety, and the safety of the public with the standard cruisers. It was on such a night that I would like to relay the story of how I broke my leg. On this night, there were a couple inches of ice and packed snow on every street. It was snowing fairly heavily, meaning there was fresh powdered snow on the ice. This is the most slippery of conditions. I remember I had walked to work that night to avoid having to find parking near the station and to limit my time driving under those awful conditions. I arrived at work and was informed that I would be doubled up in an SUV with another officer. This officer about 15 years younger than me, perhaps more, and had less than five years on the job. I took the keys to the assigned SUV and went outside to inspect the car. I noted that it had no cage, no shotgun, no computer equipment, and no medical equipment. In short, I noted that I was severely underequipped. Needless to say, my young partner and I prepared to hit the road anyway.

As we got in the car, just as I started the engine, we noted two men fighting approximately one block away. I grabbed the radio and called in the information, and began to drive toward the fight. We made no effort to rush. One of the first lessons you learn on the job is that there is no need to rush to a fist fight. It is better to conserve your energy for your arrival, to observe the situation, not rushing in blindly, plus it is to your advantage that the men involved in the fight be more tired than you when you get there. With this information in mind, we pulled up to the two combatants. It was at this point that we learned or rather observed that one of the men was an off-duty police officer who was, in fact, attempting to make an off-duty arrest. This, of course, changed the need for immediate action, and we both jumped out of the car.

I took one-step with my left foot and one with my right at which point my right foot slipped on the ice and I fell awkwardly. I heard a noise, like a dull *'thunk.'* I felt something I'm not sure what, but something in the lower part of my right leg. I attempted to regain my feet but was unable. I continued across the street, basically dragging myself by my elbows. I got to the off-duty officer, grabbed the man he was grappling with, and assisted in handcuffing him. At this point, I looked up to see my young partner standing above us and watching the action intently. I will not lie, that bothered me, and I believe he should have been a little more hands-on. I mean he didn't even hand us handcuffs, I had to retrieve them from my own belt while grappling in the snow with this drunken man.

Now, I was sitting in the snow and tried to figure out what's going on. The off-duty officer who had initiated all this explains that on his way home he was waiting to turn down the street that was blocked by a van heading up that street. The driver of the van blew his horn and made some gestures that caused the off-duty officer to exit his vehicle and confront the driver. It became immediately apparent to the off-duty officer that the driver of the van was exceptionally intoxicated. The man exited the van, the fight ensued, and that's when I arrived. A further survey of the area showed that in the van were an equally intoxicated female and two dogs.

About this time, two other officers arrived along with the city trash collector. Everyone, except me, was standing and looking around. Much to my frustration, no one took any initiative. Sitting in the snow, I contacted dispatch and requested the prisoner transportation van. I was informed that the van was unavailable. I requested any unit with the cage for the purpose of transportation. I was told that none were available. The female in the van attempted to move the van, and I yelled for officers to stop her. She was placed under arrest for driving under the influence. This simple situation had rapidly become wholly chaotic.

I called dispatch again. I told them that we needed a tow for the van, an animal control officer for the dogs, and a vehicle to transport to prisoners. Dispatch informed me that none of the things I was requesting were available. I reminded them that the situation required all of these things and requested that they make an effort in finding them. I could tell by the tone of their voice that they were becoming frustrated. Looking around the area, I realized that the city trash collector was a man whom I had known for several years. I reached up and asked him for assistance in standing. He grasped my hand and pulled me to my feet. I immediately told him to sit me back down as I could tell there was no way I was going to stand on that leg. I called dispatch yet again. The tone of their voice showed their frustration with my constant requests for assistance. I ignored this and just stated that I believe my leg was broken and requested an ambulance. This did amazing things for their attitude, and in a few moments, an ambulance was in route. By this time, a street supervisor, Sergeant, had arrived. I undid my gun belt and handed it up to him. I told him I was going to the hospital, and he said he would secure the belt in the station.

While waiting for the ambulance, I remembered something of vital importance. It had been my practice since I had gotten married to call my wife at the beginning of the shift. I would tell her that I was safe at work and in my car. This simple practice would ease her worry somewhat. I realized at this point that the chaos at the beginning of the shift had caused me to forget. So I took my phone out of my pocket and dialed my wife. And there sitting in the snow, with a broken leg, waiting for the ambulance, I told my wife one whopper of a lie.

"Hi, hun, I'm all set in my car safe and sound, I can't talk right now, it's kind of busy, but I love you and I will see you in the morning."

She replied that she loved me, told me to be careful, and hung up. This happened just as the ambulance arrived. I was loaded on a stretcher and taken to the hospital. At this point, no real pain had set in. I will say that a jolt of pain ran through my leg every time the ambulance hit a bump. The medic in the back advised me that he was going to remove my boot to get a better look. He also politely asked that I not kick him. I guess police officers make terrible patients. I did my best, well not my best, but I didn't kick him.

We arrived at the hospital, and I was taken to a room to wait for examination. A dull ache had started in my leg at this time, and I requested a Motrin, which I was given. Over the next five hours, yeah that's not a typo it took five hours, I was X-rayed, and a doctor spoke to me for about three minutes. I was informed that I had indeed broken my leg, as a matter of fact, the doctor told me I broke it well, whatever that means. I was given a temporary boot cast and crutches. During this time, several officers had stopped by to check on me. By the time I was released from the hospital, two young rookies were sent to retrieve me. One of them was the valiant young man who had watched me crawl across the street on my elbows to affect the arrest. They brought me to the station where I completed the paperwork required by my 'injured on duty status.' Those two young officers then took me home.

Getting home was a whole new adventure. On crutches and with the boot cast on, I had to climb over the snow bank, traverse an icy driveway, unlock the door, and climb three stairs to get into my kitchen. All the while these two young officers were trying desperately to help, but only managing to be in the way. It was now 5 A.M., and I knew that my coming in the house at this hour would wake and alarm my wife. I yelled and actually kicked at the younger officers to get them to go away. Once I was seated on the floor of my kitchen, I was finally able to get them to leave. I could hear my wife running down the stairs and I yelled up with, upon reflection, one of the most ridiculous things I've ever said.

"I broke my leg, I'm okay, don't come downstairs until the rookies are gone."

This injury resulted in my longest time away from the job. Healing and rehabilitation marked exactly a three-month period. That time could easily have been stretched longer, as a matter of fact, my rehabilitation therapist suggested two more weeks, but I refused. The reason I refused was that last day of physical therapy. He had me standing on my recently broken leg, on a flat piece of wood whose underside was rounded. While balancing on this half a ball, the therapist threw a small playground ball to me and had me throw it back while maintaining my balance. He was not throwing it to my chest but rather making me reach far to my left or right, up or down. After seven passes of the ball back and forth without falling, it dawned on me that I didn't know ten fully healthy officers who could do this, so I decided it was time to go back to work.

Are You Kidding?

One morning, during the summer, about one hour before the end of the shift, I was sitting in my cruiser in the back of a disused parking lot reading (probably comic books). I heard dispatch call a different car and that officer did not answer. After trying three times, dispatch called a different car, and that officer didn't answer. Dispatch again tried three times and received no answer. I am not speculating as to what those two officers were doing that they didn't answer their radio, but I will say that they were married sometime later. Dispatch called me, and I answered. I was sent to a house, and the notes of the call were that it regarded a despondent male. I remember thinking that it was an odd word to choose for such a vague call notes.

I arrived on the scene and was greeted by a young male, ushered me into the backyard saying, "Hurry, he's going to hurt someone!" I hustled into the yard and was immediately struck by the conditions back there. This yard did not seem to belong in the city, but more in a rural area. Actually, it looked like the kind of backyard where cousins 'hooked up.' There were two pickup trucks, each in a different state of disassembly. Close to my left was a complete engine block balanced atop a tree stump. I didn't have time to glance around is my attention was immediately drawn to the 'despondent male.'

Across the yard, against one of the pickups, stood a man of about my age (early 20s). He was dressed in jeans and a rather tight fitting T-shirt. His blond curly hair was unkempt. He had a hard, athletic build. He had in his hand a compound bow; and as I approached, he drew a knocked arrow, aimed at me, and said quite calmly, "Draw."

Now seems like an appropriate time to educate the reader as to the abilities and shortcomings of a Kevlar vest. The vest was designed to stop bullets. The weave of the material, when struck with force, tightens and 'catches the momentum' of the round. It was not designed for arrows. An arrow tipped with a hunting head would not be stopped by a Kevlar vest. It might slow the arrow just enough so that the fletching would get wet as they passed through me. Now, the man had a bead on me and was holding the bow at a full draw. I'm pretty fast on the draw, and pretty damned accurate once I've drawn, but there was no way I was going to break leather, draw, and aim and fire before he could let go. And even if I did manage to do all that and shoot him before he could let go he would still let go.

So I put on my best cop face, put my hands up in front of me, and attempted to talk calmly and rationally. "Hey, guy, let's settle down. We can talk about this. There's no need for this." In the meantime, I attempted to get behind the engine block as that would surely stop an arrow. As I inched my way closer to cover, the man who had greeted me in the front yard came alongside the man with the bow and snatched the arrow from the bow. I later learned that the two men were brothers. With the arrow gone, the man took on a defeated posture and rested back against the pickup, dropping the bow. His hands dropped to his side, and he slumped. Seeing this, I quickly switched gears and became the friendly officer and walked up to the man offering help and understanding. When I got within a few feet, he snapped forward and struck me in the jaw three times with rapid palm heel strikes. I fell on my ass. I popped right back up and was hit two more times, again falling on my ass. I had begun to notice a pattern forming: stand up, get hit, fall down, stand up, get hit, and fall down. I decided it was time to break that pattern. The next time I stood up, I grabbed the cuffs of his pants and dumped him on his back. (Holding my arms outstretched, thus spreading his legs, I stomped down the middle until he went limp.) I was then able to handcuff him. As I stood him up, who should arrive but the two units who had failed to answer their call. They took the prisoner from me and transported him to booking. As this happened, the man's father came out of the house, walked up to me, and placed an arm around my shoulder. What he said completely shocked me.

"Officer, I hope that some way we can overlook this."

"Are you out of your mind?" is what I attempted to say, what actually came out was a series of strange vowel noises as my jaw seemed to have stopped working. I found that by clenching my teeth, I could speak through the clench and make myself understood. "I tink my jaw is bwoken," I said.

"You're kidding me," he replied. I walked away before my temper caused more of a problem.

His wife walked out of the house and asked me, "Officer, are you all right?"

"I tink my jaw is bwoken," I replied.

"You're kidding me," she responded. I got in my car and drove off.

Arriving at the station, I was greeted by the booking sergeant who asked me what happened. Through clenched teeth, I explained the details of the call, and in response to his query as to whether I was okay, I responded, "I tink my jaw is bwoken."

Of course he replied with, "You're kidding me." I told him I would like to go to the hospital to get checked out. He agreed, of course, assuring me that the booking would be handled for me, and he even personally drove me to the hospital. At the hospital the whole "I tink my jaw is bwoken" and "you're kidding" happened three more times with each medical personnel I encountered. I began to wonder why people would think I would joke about something like this.

After a couple hours, it was announced that I had a crack/minor fracture on the thick part of my right mandible. There was no sense in wiring the jaw as it would heal without it. When the nurse came with my release papers, she told me to take my pants down. I was rather shocked by this and questioned it. She dismissed my question and asked me if I had anyone to drive me home. I was now quite sure she had the wrong patient. First, there was the whole pants issue, the second I could certainly drive. I almost never find myself in need of my jaw while driving. I don't remember exactly how I explained this to her, but I'm quite sure I was very sarcastic. She looked at me as if I were an idiot, and told me that I needed someone to drive me because she was going to give me Demerol and I couldn't drive on Demerol.

"Demerol? But Demerol is for pain."

"Well, aren't you in pain?"

"I'm uncomfortable, but I don't need Demerol."

She shrugged and walked away. I called for cruiser and went back to the station. At the station, the day shift had now taken over. The day lieutenant asked me what happened and we once again went through the entire 'kidding' scenario. The lieutenant asked me of how many days 'injured' status I had.

And I told him none. He asked why, and I said that I was fully functional and I would merely talk funny for a while. He then asked me a question I will never forget.

"What if someone else hits you?"

I went directly back to the hospital and got the doctor to sign me out injured for a few days.

I'm Still Standing

My response to the question "How are you doing?" has always been, "Well, I'm still standing; when I fall over, it's time to worry." Despite injuries and illness, and 30 years on the streets while handling other people's problems, I am still standing. This is not to say that the people of my city have not made some effort to see things otherwise. Over my career, I have been assaulted by a variety of people wielding a variety of weapons. In an earlier chapter, I mentioned a compound bow which was certainly one of the more dangerous moments. It certainly does not stand alone.

In my basement, I have a box. Actually, in my basement, I have a lot of boxes, but there is one particular that I want to talk about now. This box in my basement contains a good percentage of the weapons that I have been assaulted with over the years. My wife thinks it's morbid to hold onto these things. I keep them as a reminder of the fact that the world can change in an instant. The box is cardboard and about 4' x 4' cube. There are yards and yards of duct tape wrapped around it holding it together because the sheer weight of the objects inside has weakened its structure for years. The bottom of the box is littered with a variety of rather mundane and simple knives. If I'm honest with myself, I probably only remember 10% of the cases that some of those knives were involved in. There is one knife, however, that sticks out in my mind. It is a

87

simple serrated kitchen knife of rather cheap construction. It represents a moment on the job where I was truly afraid for my life.

I was called to a domestic argument. It was a rather busy night, and there was no backup available, so I went alone. I arrived at a three-story, six apartment building. It was not difficult to locate the cause of the disturbance as I could hear the arguing before I exited my cruiser. As I made my way to the building, I could see an open apartment door and two people inside arguing. It was a young Latino couple in their very early 20s. The argument was taking place almost exclusively in Spanish, so I did not fully understand what was going on. I could tell from her rapid speech, finger waving, and head bobbing that the female half was definitely furious. The male half was backpedaling and appeared to be apologizing. I entered the apartment and got between the two and attempted to calm things down. Thankfully, they both spoke English, and I was able to communicate with them. The man was thin with long black hair pulled tight in a ponytail. He seemed rather afraid and almost thankful for my presence. The female half remained highly agitated. She was dressed in pajama pants and a tank top T-shirt, her hair was a mess, and it was evident that she had woken up only recently.

While the male half of this argument claimed to have no idea why his woman was so upset, the female was more than happy to explain to me what was going on. She explained to me that she was awoken by a phone call from her sister who had seen her new husband out dancing with another girl at a club. The focal point of her anger was not so much that he was dancing with another girl or even the implied infidelity. Her true anger seemed to be focused on the fact that this girl was a blond. I had no success in calming her down, and at one point, she turned and picked up the kitchen knife I mentioned. She held it firmly in her right fist and stepped towards her hapless husband. Unfortunately for me, I was between them. I drew my sidearm but did not point at her. I kept it aimed at the floor between us and begged her to drop the knife. She looked at me and said quite clearly words that I will remember on my deathbed.

"I am going to cut his balls off. If I have to cut yours off to get to him, I will."

With that, I trained my gun on her and again begged her to drop the knife so that I would not have to shoot her. She looked at the gun and appeared to see it for the first time. I suppose that in her rage she was just not paying attention to the situation around her as she was so focused on the man cowering behind me. She was arrested and booked without incident. Once the object of her rage—her husband—was removed from her site, she calmed immediately and apologized profusely to me.

Sticking out of the box right next to the compound bow is an item that truly seems out of place. It is a 3½ foot all aluminum mountain climbers pickaxe. This is an article which is exactly what it sounds like—a device that is used by climbers to scale icy heights. I can only assume that this item found its way to my city as a means of removing ice from a commercial fishing boat. Regardless of how it found its way into my city, it found its way into my possession in a rather comical manner. One day while investigating a disturbance, I discovered that one of the men involved had warrants. While placing him under arrest for those warrants, I evidently incurred the wrath of his grandmother. While I was escorting this large hairy biker to my cruiser for transport, I saw an amazing sight. Coming around from the back of the house was a 90-year-old woman. She was gray, not just her hair, but all of her. She wore a faded housecoat and surprisingly brand-new expensive running shoes. She wasn't moving very quickly, but she was heading for me and holding the pickaxe above her head, she announced her intention to free her grandson. She was so terribly old and slow that I was able to walk up to her and take it from her hands without further incident. I threw the pickaxe into the trunk of my car and completely ignored the incident. I kept the pickaxe as a trophy, but there was no way I was going to arrest this 80-pound woman for assaulting me.

In the corner of the box strapped together are a half-dozen homemade, 'medieval' style weapons. There is a studded club, a mace, a flail, and a battle-axe. I wasn't assaulted with any of these in particular, but they were confiscated by me from a group of teenagers. This group of teenagers was marching from their neighborhood to a rival neighborhood for what I could only assume was the beginning of the siege. They gave up the weapons and went home rather easily after I explained that each and every item was an arrestable offence, just for carrying it. These pretend tough guys never really put me in fear, nor did they assault me. But those were weapons certainly make interesting trophies.

The last item of particular interest in my box of doom is a meat cleaver. Not just any meat cleaver but a two-handed monster with a 3-foot handle and a 2½-foot head. The whole thing weighs more than 25 pounds. It is rusted and probably over 100 years old. I don't know where it came from, but when I encountered it, it was in the hands of a very crazy man. The man was out on the street waving this meat cleaver around and insisting that a woman was being raped on top of the next building. Once we were able to get the cleaver away from him and arrest this man for the public disturbance he had created, we actually drove him up the street to an area where the roof of the building he spoke of could be observed. There we pointed out to him that there was no one on the roof. I don't know if his insanity was genetic or drug-induced. All I do know was if this large muscle-bound man had connected as he swung that cleaver toward me, I would be missing body parts.

Who Would Do That
on Purpose?

Working the midnight shift for the majority of my career has left me with a very low threshold for stupidity. I think it has something to do with the absolute tidal wave of stupid that comes at me on a nightly basis. There are two choices when there is that much stupid. You can either develop a high tolerance for it, and pretty much ignore it, or you can snap back with the sarcasm that borders on rude. Okay, it steps well over the line into rude. At least it does in my case.

As an example, one of the many jobs I have performed for my department has been that of the background investigator. All potential officers are screened by a trained investigator before any physical or psychological examination. Part of my duties as a background investigator was to greet the candidates and supervise the filling out of their applications. I could not help but sitting in the room watching them fill out an 11-page application that my life one day might very well depend on some of these people. That thought actually frightened me.

I remember one instance in particular. I remember the candidate was male. I remember he was 24 years old. I remember his name was Lance. (Seriously, Lance? I sincerely hope it was a family name.) Lance was seated in the back of the room and raised his hand to ask a question. I acknowledged him and asked him what he wanted. He said, "I have a question regarding number 12." I picked up a blank application and read number 12.

12. Have you ever been in a motor vehicle accident in which you were the driver?

Now, this seems like a relatively straightforward question, and I couldn't imagine what was causing Lance difficulty and I expressed this much to him. I did tell him to go ahead with this question.

"I hit a tree, does that count?"

"Well, let's see, first when you hit the tree, were you in a car?"

"Yes."

"Were you driving the car?"

"Yes."

"Third, and most important, did you hit the tree on purpose?"

"No."

"Then it was an accident. Write it down."

I believe, but I'm not certain, that was the third time I was spoken to by the captain about being nicer to the recruits. As a side note, Lance was not selected for the job. He was a fine candidate, but we just did not reach his number, and he never applied again. I hope it wasn't due to my treatment of him, but if I'm honest with myself, it was probably a factor.

Many Parts Make a Cop, Not All Are Visible

During my stint as a background investigator, I believe I became a much better police officer. I learned many valuable skills, specifically in the area of interviews. The job also taught me to be self-motivating and to work almost completely independent of supervision. For the most part, the job was rather easy, the reasons to bypass a candidate are quite specific and laid out. If we had a reason to bypass someone, we did; and if we did not, then we did not. Just because the rules were cut and dry, does not mean the job was.

In one particular instance, I was assigned the investigation of the candidate who was in his early 30s. He was a little overweight, and one could tell that this was due to a lack of physical activity. He had a soft appearance about him. This man's background was impeccable. He had never been arrested, or even the subject of an investigation. He had never been fired from a job, nor even reprimanded at any of his employments. His neighbors loved him and spoke highly of his caring nature. The problem that I had with this candidate was that without exception, every person I talked to said something to the effect of, "I can't believe he is going to be a police officer. He is so timid." This was disturbing to me as I did not want my backup to be someone who would freeze up under stress. I approach my sergeant, asked him for advice on the matter. He told me what I already knew that there was nothing to bypass the man on. However, he agreed to sit in with me on my final interview with him.

On the day of the interview, the candidate arrived wearing a flannel shirt, jeans, and sneakers. He looked a little unkempt and casual for such an interview. I sat him in an empty classroom and left him alone for about 15 minutes. At that time, the sergeant and I entered the room. The room had those full-length swinging doors which allowed us to enter side-by-side, and push the doors quickly. As we walked in the candidate looked up at us wide-eyed and exclaimed, "Wow!" We asked him what he thought warranted such an exclamation. He replied that he thought we were very intimidating. I let that go, and we commenced with the interview. There were several points in his application that required clarification. There was nothing of consequence, just missing dates, blank spaces, and other small things of that nature. Typically, the interview would move forward at a conversational pace, however, in this instance, the sergeant and I threw questions at him rapid-fire. We could see the stress levels rising, and at one point, early on in the interview, he clutched onto his cheek. Let me make this clear, he grabbed his cheek with all five fingers, and squeezed his hand into a fist digging his nails in. A quick glance at the sergeant told me he had also seen this, but we chose not to mention it.

The questioning moved away from his application and now focused on his rather obvious discomfort. I asked him to tell me what he felt the tension in the room was on a scale of 1 to 10. He replied, "Oh God, it's a 10, maybe even an 11." (I would have given him bonus points for a spinal tap reference, but I sincerely don't believe that was his intention.) I pointed out to him that he was in no danger; no one in the room had threatened him, nor acted aggressively towards him. I pointed out that the sergeant and I had placed our guns in the secure locker, we were not even armed. Background investigations are a plain clothed assignment, so we were not in uniform. We were in a large, well lit room, and there was a large table between him and us. Bearing all that in mind, if this is a 10 or perhaps an 11, what happens on the street when he's outnumbered? More importantly, what happens on the street when *I'm* outnumbered and I need his help? I asked if he would be able to overcome his apparent anxiety to come to my assistance. He responded that he would, but the quiver in his voice told everyone in the room including him, otherwise.

At this point, I took a piece of tissue and I handed to him. I asked him to place it up against his cheek. He did, and when I told him to take his hand away, the paper stayed. When he reached up to remove the paper, he saw that it was soaked through with blood. In his tension and anxiety, he had squeezed his cheek so very hard, that he had clawed himself open. He stared at the tissue open-mouthed. I let him be quiet for a moment and I asked for his thoughts on what he saw. He said that he didn't know what say. It was evident that he was as dumbfounded by what happened as we were. I then told him about his investigation, and how almost every person that I spoke with to include the people he had put down as references had questioned his ability to be a police officer due to his timid nature.

I told him that the interview was over. I said that on all 'technical' merits he was a viable candidate. I told him that on the following day I would move his application forward, and he would next meet with the captain's board to get their recommendation. This would be held in the very same room, but instead of meeting with a sergeant and me, he would meet with three captains, and the process would be repeated. The captains would most likely have their own series of questions, and those questions would at least, in part, come from my report of the interview today. I told him to go home. I told him to find some quiet, alone time. I asked him to seriously consider whether or not he truly wanted this job, and to consider, most importantly, if he could truly do this job. I reminded him that it was not just his safety there was of concern but that of the people around him and his fellow officers.

The following day, he dropped off a letter at the main desk. The letter was very nicely written, polite, and apologetic. He respectfully withdrew his application and thanked everyone for their efforts. To this day, I believe I acted in the best interest of that applicant and the department. He was a good and honorable man. He was smart and had compassion. Those things alone, however, are not enough. You have to have the ability to act under pressure, not freeze. I hope he's done well since then. I hope he found his place.

Never Forget a Sunrise

Working the majority of my career on the midnight to eight shifts, I have seen far more sunrises than most people. I consider myself rather lucky in this respect. In the spring and summer, the sun rising has been one of my favorite sights over the years, and I have often contemplated my luck at having been able to view them. Most people greet the new day by opening their eyes and rising from their beds. Perhaps, they open a blind to see the world lit by the sun and already active. I have been lucky enough to watch the night sky turn into the day as the art show that is a New England sunrise opens before me. I have watched the world wake up many times and thought to myself that the people waking up consider this the beginning of the day. I consider this because I know the day began long before they open their eyes. I also know that these people who are greeting their day got through the night because my brother and sister officers watched over them as they slept.

I do truly love sunrises, but they are not the only things that have greeted my eyes at that hour of the day. I have seen some truly amazing things. There is a saying, I'm not sure, but I think it's a joke more than a saying, but just about everyone has heard of the 'walk of shame.' It probably has its origins in the college setting. To my understanding, it refers to a woman, or young girl returning home in the daylight still dressed in her club clothes from the night before. Whenever I hear this phrase, I always picture a young blond girl in her little black dress. Her hair is a mess, her makeup is smeared, and she is carrying her high-heeled shoes as she makes her way back to her dorm room. I have seen many women, and more than a few men who are obviously on their 'walk of shame.' These things usually happen right around that great sunrise hour.

One morning, I was in a park. It is one of my favorite places to be at the sunrise hour. It is at a very high point in the city in the open field in front allows for a spectacular view eastward. On a particular morning in mind, I was driving through the park, looking to select a spot to see my sunrise. I noticed a car parked near the pond. It is not unusual to see cars parked in this location at this time of day. People will often walk or run around the park in the mornings. This was a very beautiful early summer day, and I initially thought nothing of the car parked by the pond. I simply figured that someone was getting an early start. As I drove past the car, my attention was drawn to someone making a quick movement opposite the car from me. I saw a figure in a flowery sundress with long black hair ducking and circling the car to keep the car between them and me. I did not know if someone was in trouble or causing trouble, but I decided to investigate.

I stop my cruiser and exited. I called out, asking whoever was there if they were okay and if they needed help. The figure very quickly ran around the car, opened the door, and entered as I walked up to knock on the window the engine started, and the car sped off. As the car sped off, dozens of ducks scattered to avoid being struck. Some of them took to the air while others waddled quickly to the water. One of the ducks actually flew up past my face and knocked my hat off. I recovered quickly jumped back in my cruiser and gave chase to the vehicle, activating my lights and siren. The chase led throughout the city and probably totaled about 10 miles. The car sped around circling blocks and doubling back. In all, we ended up less than a mile from where we started. Several officers joined the chase with me, and when the car finally pulled over, we surrounded the car with me at the driver's window. I could now see that the driver was a man in his early 40s. He had locked the car's doors and was refusing to acknowledge our presence. Now at this point, because of the chase and his initial refusal to stop, the driver was under arrest. After a few minutes of trying to get him to open the door, the street sergeant gave me the order to break the window and get him out of the car. I pulled out my department, issued nightstick, and struck the window twice, completely failing to break the window. As I prepared to make a third strike, the man exited the car and placed his hands in the air. He was now dressed only in a pair of underwear. The underwear was cotton and could have been described as 'granny panties.' In the car, we found the wig and the sundress. It appears that during the 10-mile chase through the neighborhoods, he had managed to take off the wig and sundress without crashing.

When the court day came, and this man had to answer to the charges, he initially wanted to make an excuse that he was not wearing his proper glasses and therefore did not know it was a police officer who approached them in the park or chased him through the city. I spoke with the district attorney and asked if I might meet with this gentleman's attorney. This is rather unusual; however, the defense attorney agreed to meet with me. I told him that I was unaware of how much his client informed him of that day. I said that if we go to trial, he should know that one of the first questions asked of me is going to be, what initially drew my attention on that day. I then laid out for the attorney exactly what I saw and what happened. Very shortly after that, after consultation with his client, the defense attorney informed the court that they would be pleading guilty to all charges.

It occurred to me sometime later that all the ducks that were surrounding the man's car were some distance from the water and at a spot where ducks do not usually congregate. I questioned the duck's activity in my mind, however, I never actually understood it. I have discussed this with many people over the years as I've told my stories and one gentleman informed me that the egg channel of a duck is very similar to a woman's vagina. I am not by any means speculating that this man was molesting the ducks. I have though, often giggled to myself thinking about holding a stuffed duck and asking the collection at the pond, "Where did the bad man touch you?"

The park where I enjoy my sunrises, in addition to the duck pond, also contains the zoo. I love the zoo; every year I buy a membership. I will often walk through the zoo after my morning run as a cool down. One summer morning several years before the 'duck incident,' I was in the field, parked facing east, watching my sunrise. I was not asleep, or at least I don't think I was, but I definitely was not paying attention to what was going on. I was very young on the job at the time. I was looking to make as few waves as possible as I was still in the learning phase. As I looked east and watched the city wake up, there was some movement to my left. I turned and in stunned silence watched as three elephants walked past my cruiser. There are, in fact elephants at the zoo. However, these elephants were out in an open field. My initial thought was to call in and get some help. I had concluded that the elephants had somehow escaped their enclosure and I was going to have to once again deal with something the Academy had not trained me to do. I hesitated because I knew that putting this out on the air would label me 'the elephant man,' for the rest of my career. Just as I grabbed the microphone, I noticed several zoo employees were walking beside the elephants, calmly.

I spoke with them (from some distance) and learned that they often take the elephants for walks at that hour. They did this to let the elephants out of their small enclosure and stretch their legs. I am thrilled that I hesitated, and did not call that in. I am also happy that the situation happened, because since that time, whenever possible, I get to that spot at that hour of the morning and watch the elephants go for a walk.

I Would Rather Be Rich Than Good Looking
(Crap, Is There a Third Option?)

The vast majority of my career has been spent in Uniformed Patrol. I honestly feel that that was where I belong. I know that that is where I've done the most good. Lastly, I believe that there is where I was able to guide many young officers and help them over some rough spots early in their careers. That is not saying that I did not try other aspects of the job. I spent almost four years as a detective. To clarify, in my department, detective is not a rank but merely a job description/assignment. Going to detectives is not a promotion, simply a change of duties. As a matter of fact, an officer often finds that his salary takes quite a hit as a result of being assigned to the detective division. First, there is the loss of any night differential pay. Second, as court is held during the day hours, it almost never results in overtime for the detectives. Lastly, all the really well-paying details happened during the day. It is not uncommon for a detective to make $10,000 less his first year as a detective than he did the previous year.

One day, I was in the office while making some calls and polishing up some reports. There were two other detectives in the office with me, along with the secretary. The office was on the second floor of our original police headquarters, which had been built in the early 1800s. To the best of my knowledge, that office had always been the Detective Division. Hell, I even had a roll top desk that I know was close to a century old. The two detectives were both men of about my age at the time. That is to say, we were all in our mid-20s. The secretary was much older, not quite as old as my desk, but I bet she remembered it when it still looked new. She had gray hair that she wore in tight curls. She dressed in a smart business suit with skirt and jacket. She wore that clunky jewelry that was so popular in the 40s and 50s. She was old enough that she no longer walked but shuffled her feet. I honestly think that she had relatives within the higher ranks of the department, and that's how she was able to keep working past her level of efficiency

A phone call came in; she took a message and looked about the room. She got up and shuffled over to Detective G., he was in his early 20s, with brown wavy hair and model looks. She presented him the message; he looked it over and told her that it was not his case. She shuffled across the room, it was a big room, and it took a while, and presented the note to Detective M., a classmate of mine from the Academy. He was a short fellow of thin build with a winning smile. He was usually the best-dressed man in the office. He also looked over the note and told her that it was not his case either. She sat back down at her desk and went about her work. A few minutes later, Detective W, a tall stocky individual with broad shoulders and wavy black hair, walked into the room. As he sat at his desk, the secretary climbed to her feet and made her way to present him with a note. He looked it over and said that he didn't know who the woman was that the note referred to. The secretary turned around and went back to her desk. I believe that it is worth noting that on two of her three trips to the office the secretary had to pass directly by my desk.

My curiosity got the better of me. I'd seen this message get passed from person to person, and I wanted to know what was on it. I asked the secretary what that was all about. She stated, "This woman called and said she had spoken with a detective today, she says she doesn't know his name, she only remembers that he was really **good-looking**." It dawned on me at this point that, while looking for a 'good-looking' detective, the secretary had passed that note to every man working the office that day, every man except me. Choosing not to bring that point out (the giggles from the other detectives told me I didn't have to), I asked what the woman's name was. She told me, and I informed her that it was, in fact, my case. (Despite her evaluation of my looks.)

He Is Just a Boy

If you know a police officer, and you've known him or her for a long time, particularly since before they became a police officer, you may have noticed a change in their demeanor. You may notice that their capacity for sympathy has been significantly reduced. I know this to be true about myself. The mental image that I have of myself is of a caring man capable of empathy and compassion. Being honest with myself, however, I know the things that I've seen and the people I've dealt with have diminished these capabilities. The following is an example of the story that comes to mind whenever I feel like being lenient.

I was working in the detective division and I was recently promoted from property crime to the violent crime division. Promotion is a relative term as there is no change in rank or pay, only the nature of crimes you are assigned to. I was working on a series of purse snatchings. All of the victims in my folder were women over the age of 60. A number of them had been injured when they were robbed. Based on initial descriptions of the suspect, it was believed that one man was responsible for five different purse snatchings. Based on the description of the man, the area in which the robberies had occurred, and the direction in which the suspect fled after each robbery, I developed a series of suspects. I put together a photo array of eight suspects and visited each victim in turn. Four out of the five victims immediately and positively identified one particular male. The fifth victim was over 90 years old and due to her poor eyesight was unable to make an identification.

I obtained a warrant for the rest of this male based on the investigation and proceeded to his home. The suspect, in this case, was a 17-year-old man who lived with his mother. When I executed the search warrant, he was not at home; however, in searching his room, three purses, as well as personal items from my victims, were located. A short time later, this young man was found and arrested. During his booking and subsequent interviews, he denied everything and made no statements. Updated photos of him were taken, and each victim was re-interviewed. The results were the same as the initial investigation in that the same for women identified him as the man who had robbed and injured them. Taking into account the violent nature of his crimes, I requested a high cash bail so that he would be held until trial. This all happened on a Friday.

That Sunday, the local newspaper ran an article that was one and a half pages long and included a photo of the young man that had been provided by his mother. The photo was from when he was 12 years old and portrayed him as an innocent child. The article went on to imply that this child should not be held in an adult prison. It quoted him as being afraid of the other prisoners and recounted his allegations of their threats to do him harm. The article named me specifically as the investigating detective who had requested the high cash bail which was keeping this child in prison. I took no personal offense to this, as the media, specifically, newsprint have often taken the side which paints police officers as beasts.

That Monday morning, I believe because of the newspaper article, the young suspect was granted a bill review, and within 15 minutes of appearing before the judge was released on his

107

own personal recognizance. I later learned that he and his mother walked out of the courthouse after his release; and before they left the parking lot, he had walked away from his mother. A short time later, a call came in for a woman who had been knocked down and had her purse stolen. Sitting in the office, I heard the case and I immediately rushed to the hospital to interview the victim. I brought with me the original photo array, along with the updated photos. Once the hospital staff agreed to let me interview the victim, I stepped into the room where she was being treated. I recall this woman was 71 years old and probably weighed less than 100 pounds. The attack which resulted in her purse being stolen had fractured her collarbone and dislocated her elbow. I was lucky that I had arrived before her being given any pain medications as that might have tainted her identification. I presented her with the photo array, and she immediately identified the suspect as the man who hurt and robbed her.

It took me two hours to locate him, but I found the suspect again. Upon placing him under arrest, I found in his pocket a checkbook and other personal items belonging to my victim. It took him less than ten minutes after being released to find another victim, rob, and injure her. After completing the arrest and shipping this male back to court, I contacted the newspaper. I spoke specifically with the reporter who had written the article. I asked her if she would like to write a follow-up article based on this new information because she seemed so vested in the original story. She hung up on me and refused to take any more of my calls.

Sometimes, I may come across as very uncaring and without compassion. It is because of this and similar cases, that crossed my mind whenever I feel the urge to be lenient.

Domestic Violence

When I first started on the job, the domestic violence laws were not yet in place. Domestic violence calls were a point of frustration because of some of the limitations the laws have in place. Simple assault and battery, that is to say, a punch in the face, is not an arrestable offense if it does not happen in the officer's presence. If two men get into a fight outside of a bar, and upon the officer's arrival both men admit to punching one another, but the fight is over, the officer does not have the ability to arrest those men. Before the domestic violence laws were in place, a domestic fight was, unfortunately, treated much the same manner. Arriving at a home and seeing a woman with a bloody nose, an officer would have almost no recourse even if she told the police that her husband punched her, and her husband admitted to hitting her on the scene.

In situations such as this, we would do our utmost to find a way to separate the two. We would suggest that the husband take a walk and cool off. We might suggest he stay at a friend or relative's home for the night to allow things to relax. This was very often met with aggressive argument. The man would often state that it was his home and he would be damned if he were going to leave. We would then have to turn to the woman, the victim in the matter, and ask her if she had someplace that she could go to be safe for the night. We did not like this. We understood that we were re-victimizing the woman. We knew that making her leave her home after she had been assaulted was not right. We had little in our power to rectify this. I would on occasion such as this often become rather insulting and aggressive towards the man. I would insinuate that he was a coward and unable to fight a man. I would say that he was less than a man for striking a woman. I would say all these things in the hopes of provoking him to assault me. This would have given me the ability to arrest him and solve the situation for the night. Sometimes this worked, sometimes it didn't.

The domestic violence laws made the assault and battery of a household member and arrestable offense, even if it happened before the police arrived. We now had the ability to make the arrest based on the evidence at hand. This solved a lot of problems. This has been a perfect law, and I am a supporter.

Like all things, there are ways to corrupt and abuse the situation. Many women lie to have their husband or boyfriend arrested when they are angry with him. There are women who wait for the fishing fleet to come in, knowing the fisherman are loaded with cash. They will stay with and party with these fishermen until the money is gone. They will then call in a domestic assault, and I will have to lock up a man who has likely done nothing but spend his money. I would like to say again that I do not believe that the domestic violence law is a bad thing in any way. I would just say that, like anything, it has often been abused and perverted for some people's own purpose.

There was one instance before the domestic violence laws where my taunting strategy worked. I was working with Officer G. We arrived on scene for a domestic violence call. We met a young woman outside who explained that her husband had beaten her up. Everything we could see about this woman certainly made her story seem truthful. Her face was bruised, bloody, and swollen. She told us that this man, her husband, was still inside and that she had fled out the back door when she saw the police arriving. We went inside and confronted this gentleman about the assault on his wife. It didn't take much in the way of provoking because this gentleman was itching to fight from the first moment we walked in. He was a huge and muscular man. Between Officer G and me, we were able to subdue him, but it took the better part of ten minutes. It was quite literally a knockdown, drag out fight. Furniture was broken. Uniforms were ruined. In the end, the man was arrested, and we guided him out of the house.

As we still were walking him to the cruiser, the female complainant ran up to us. We turned to face her with the defendant between us. She asked us how much bail would be. Officer G and I looked at each other stunned. I explained to her about the fee for bail and that it was $25. She looked in her purse, and I could see that there were two tens and a five in her purse. I was just about to explain to her that she could not do this here it had to be done at the station. As I began my explanation, she placed her purse over her shoulder, reached back far behind her, and let fly an amazing punch. It was a right-handed haymaker that connected directly with her husband's cheek. She was a petite girly girl. I don't believe there was much behind her punch, but we stood in shock that someone had just punched our prisoner as he stood between us. This little blond girl then turned around and placed her hands behind her back. Initially, we thought she wanted to bail her husband out. In reality, she was making sure she had enough bail money for herself so that she could punch him and let her frustrations out. I made the arrest, I had too. I didn't like it.

There was one couple who I dealt with on a number of occasions. They were married but separated. There was a restraining order in effect. This order was a long-term and complicated order that involved children and visitation. The order itself had a 'no contact' section to it. This means that contacting the plaintiff, in this case, the female, was an arrestable offense for the defendant, in this case, the male. Because child visitation was involved, certain stipulations were added. In this particular case, on Saturday mornings at 7 o'clock, the mother would drive the children to a particular street corner. She would drop them off and then back away 50 yards. (The distance specified in the order.) The father would then drive up to pick up the children, and the process would be reversed on Sunday evening.

One particular Saturday morning, in the middle of winter, it was snowing horribly. The father in this particular case could not manage to get his car started. He called the mother to tell her to not bring the children to the corner. He explained that he could not start his vehicle, and he did not want the children to wait on the corner. This was the sum total of the conversation. The mother, after finishing this conversation on the phone, called the police. I arrived, and she explained about the order, and about the phone call. She explained that she knew how the order worked quite well and that I was to arrest this man for calling her in violation of the order. I asked a few questions that I felt were pertinent. I asked if during the phone call he had been insulting, threatening, or in any way abusive. She said that he had not, and accused me of not wanting to make the arrest because "all you men stick together."

I went to the home of the father and found him attempting to get the car started. I asked him about the situation and if he understood about the order and its 'no contact' paragraph. He stated that he understood but that did not want the children to stand in the snow for no reason. He was calm and perfectly reasonable. Even when I informed him that I had to place him under arrest for the violation of the order, he stated he understood and came along quietly. I do not know the history of these people. The man, in this case, may have been a brutal lunatic. On the day that I dealt with them, however, the woman was accusatory and angry and vindictive. The man was cooperative and quiet. I did my job. I didn't like it.

One night, I was sent on a domestic call. The call came from neighbors who stated that there was a very loud argument between a man and a woman at the house next door. I arrived on scene and knocked on the door. I heard a male voice tell me to come in. I opened the door, identified myself, and entered the house. Looking around, I made several observations. The first thing that I noted was that the male was wearing jeans, but nothing else no shirt, no shoes. His nose appeared to be broken, and he had bruises and scratch marks all over his upper torso. Beside him, where he sat, was a table and on that table was a birthday cake. It was summer time and very humid, and the frosting on the cake had melted. It was actually a bit of a sad sight. I asked the man to tell me what happened. He explained that it was his wife's birthday and that he had purchased a cake at about 4 o'clock in the afternoon when he knew she was due home from work. She had not arrived home until about 2 o'clock in the morning. When she walked in the door, she was drunk and had explained to him that she decided to go two states over to get a tattoo with 'the guys from work.' He explained that he had wished that she had let him know, so he did not wait up or worry. He told me that when he said this, she became enraged and began to punch him. I asked him if he hit her back and he looked at me shocked.

"No, no way. I would never hit a woman. That is just not right."

At this point, the wife stepped out of a back room. I had no idea that she was still on scene, the male seemed so calm and despondent. She stepped out of the back room completely naked. She was a tall, attractive woman with long black hair. She had a shapely body. I know this because every bit of it was on display, including the new tattoo. It was a tribal band around her ankle. I asked her to tell me what happened. Much to my surprise, she reiterated her husband's story almost word for word. She told me that she went for the tattoo. She said she didn't call him because she felt she didn't have to. She said that when he complained that she hadn't called, he sounded like a pussy. She explained that she punched him and scratched him. I asked her if he ever hit her back. She said that he had not because he was such a wimp. She then stood, naked, fists on hips, for all the world resembling a naked Wonder Woman, and said, "Now, arrest him."

I was momentarily stunned. I was not expecting this at all. I asked her what she thought I should arrest him for. She looked at me as though I were stupid, reassumed her fists on hips pose and this time actually glanced up towards the ceiling as she exclaimed, "You can't arrest me, I'm the woman."

I asked her as politely as I could to please get dressed. When she asked why, I explained to her that she was an exceptionally lovely young lady and that seeing her naked was making me uncomfortable. She seemed to believe this and got dressed. When she was dressed, I arrested her for the domestic assault. She laughed at me throughout the entire booking process because she thought that I was going to be fired. She explained that any cop dumb enough to arrest a woman in a domestic case was too stupid to be a cop and would be fired. That was nearly 20 years ago, and I haven't been fired. I guess her theory was flawed.

I Always Wanted to Be Cool

Note: The following story contains some exceptionally harsh and vulgar language. I apologize for this. However, it is necessary for an authentic retelling.

On a hot summer night, I was dispatched to a call. The notes of the call were that an exceptionally intoxicated male was walking along the middle of the main street. Nine times out of 10, calls of this nature result in nothing. By the time the caller phones in the information, the call taker enters the information, and the dispatcher gives it out, the drunk has usually moved on. That was not the case in this instance. I arrived at the area designated in the call, and sure enough, a man was walking down the center of the street. For every step forward he took, he then took one to the side to steady himself. I pulled over exited my car and spoke to him. He showed every outward sign of exceptional intoxication.

I asked him to step to the side of the road so we wouldn't be hit but traffic, and he complied. I asked him to sit in my car, assuring him I would not lock him in, again he complied. I asked him where he lived and he gave me an address that was less than two blocks away. I told him that I was going to check in for warrants and if he had none, I would give him a ride home. He responded by saying, "You're cool." (I'm cool? That's awesome. I always wanted to be cool.) I called in his information, and he had five warrants. I informed him that he was under arrest for these warrants, and suddenly, I wasn't cool anymore.

It now becomes necessary, for the sake of this story, to explain that I am a white male officer, and this gentleman was black. I avoid in the telling of my stories race and gender if they have no place. In this instance, however, is necessary to explain the story fully.

As I transported this gentleman to booking, he transformed from a happy, singing type drunk, to an angry and foul-mouthed drunk. In addition to spitting at me through the screen between the seats (we did not yet have Plexiglas), my prisoner informed me of the following.

"You are only arresting me because I am black. You are prejudiced. I can tell because all white motherfuckers with short hair are prejudiced." The irony of that statement was not lost on me. To be honest, I laughed so hard I had to pull over for a moment. His response to my pulling over was, "Oh, so now you're going to beat me up." (I didn't.) Once I got to booking, my prisoner showed me that he was no stranger to this game. He immediately informed my supervisor that he was only arrested because the officer is prejudiced and he is black. He also claimed to have chest pains, knowing this would earn him a trip to the hospital rather than jail. Booking someone with warrants is a rather quick task. I had it completed by the time the ambulance had him aboard. I rode with my prisoner to the hospital in the ambulance.

Once at the hospital, my prisoner continued to spew anger and vulgarities. He shouted out the following so loudly that he had to be moved away from other patients.

"I'm going to kill you! I'm going to kill your family…I'm going to burn down your house. I'm going to rape your children!"

The nurse in the room looked at me with sympathy. I believe she felt that this man's tirade was somehow hurting me. It wasn't. I had long since disregarded anything that came out of his mouth as the ranting of a foolish man. My sarcasm, however, could not be contained. I replied with the following:

"No, no, no, you have this all wrong. If you kill me first, how will I know you've done any of the other things? If you kill my family first, then you can't rape my children. That would be necrophilia, not rape. If you set the house on fire, then you have to rush through the rape, and you won't be able to enjoy yourself. So here's what you do. First rape the children, take your time and really enjoy yourself. Then kill my family, leaving me alive. Then set the house on fire. And lastly, kill me, that way I witness all of it before I die."

I said all of this as matter-of-factly and as calmly as I would had I been giving instructions to assembling a bicycle or directions to a restaurant. My reply to his rant had two wonderful effects. First, it shut him the hell up, and second, it brought about a look of utter shock upon the nurse that I will remember to the day I die. Even writing this now, I am giggling to myself at her stunned expression.

What the Hell Happened Here?

Two of the most horrific car accidents that I have ever witnessed involved Chevy Camaro's. Each was a single car crash, and each resulted in a fatality. They each happened during different stages of my career. One very early on and the other around the ten-year mark, at a point in my time when I was entrusted with the training of rookies.

The first happened on a stretch of secondary highway that splits the city. As this highway goes through the downtown area, it has an S curve. It is well known that you can take this S-curve of the rather high rate of speed if you time it just right. On this night, someone did not time it correctly. I was about a mile away when I heard another cruiser call off the crash. In his panic, that officer's voice betrayed his lack of composure. I remember very specifically that he used the words, 'possible DOA.' I raced to the scene using blue lights and siren. (To some degree we all took the job to drive fast and make noise.) I arrived on scene, and it took me several minutes to discern what it happened.

It appeared as though the Camaro was attempting to negotiate the S-curve at a very high rate of speed. The driver was unable to maintain control, went into a slide, and struck the guardrail. The striking of the guardrail sent the car into a tumble, and the driver was ejected. He landed on the guardrail, and the car landed on him and rolled off. When I say roll, I do not mean on its tires, but it was flipping. When I first looked at the man lying in the street, it took a few moments to process what I was looking at. The first thing I noted was a fist-sized hole in his chest which had likely come from a disastrous impact with the steering column. I then noticed that his left femur was broken and had pushed through both his skin and the fabric of his jeans. I next noticed that his left foot wasn't there. It had been severed just above the ankle. I observed a pinkish material that looked like flesh protruding from his mouth and nose. I later learned that this was the inner workings of his lungs which had been forced out from the impact to his chest. My last observation was that none of these wounds were bleeding With this meant to me was that this man's heart was not pumping and there nothing 'possible' about his death. It was a certainty.

I learned a few things from that accident. I found out that looking for a foot along the highway is a very distasteful task. I learned that it is not quite as unpleasant as finding a foot along the road. (It was still in the sneaker.) I found out that I positively hate 'gawkers,' people standing by watching as this poor soul has carted away in pieces. Lastly, I learned that this young man was the son of one of the senior members of the department. I stood by and watched with horrific sadness when the patrol captain brought the dead young man's father to the scene. I looked at a man who I knew is tough as nails, a veteran officer, a man feared and respected on the street not only for a long and storied career but for his absolute no-nonsense attitude. I watched him break down and cry. A one-car crash fatality leaves very little as far as police work goes. There is no one to charge. There is no one to interview. There are no citations to write. All you can do is write up an accident report stating the facts as best that you can, and this, as clinically as you can.

The other horrific accident happened about ten years later. I remember that on that night I had a very young officer with me. He was a tall, thin, good-looking kid. He wore his black hair in a spike manner that was popular at the time. I remember that this kid was academically brilliant. I enjoyed working with him. We had great conversations. We were dispatched to an accident along a secondary highway that passes east and west through the city. The accident had occurred in a business district that resembled a strip mall.

After my initial report, an accident reconstruction team had been dispatched to clarify and verify what it happened. Based on skid marks, and other measurements they determined at the time of the crash the car had been traveling more than 110 miles an hour. This car was also a Chevy Camaro. When we first arrived on scene, the chaos we were presented with was difficult to fathom. Two-thirds of the car, everything from the firewall back, was lying on its side in the middle of the parking lot. The driver had evidently just picked up a lot of dry-cleaning as there were clothes strewn everywhere. I'm not exaggerating when I say there were at least three dozen shirts, on hangers, and in dry cleaner bags. The shirts were cast about in a roughly circular pattern at least 40 yards across. The front half of the car (that is to say from the firewall forward, including the steering wheel, dashboard, and engine) was about 50 yards away from the rest of the car. I remember noting that the headlights were still on.

While I was taking in the scene, I glanced over at my rookie. His eyes were as large as saucers, and his mouth hanging agape. He was turning in a small circle. It looked for

121

as if someone had nailed the toe of his left boot to the ground as he just continually pivoted and took in the scene. What was most troubling initially was that there were two parts of a car, and a lot the clothing, but no person. I shook the rookie, snapped him out of his shock, and got him searching the area. A few moments later by the front half of the car, I found the man who had been driving. It was a small man who appeared to be of Latin American descent, most likely Guatemalan or Honduran. I had found him with the front half of the car. It seemed that at the impact he held on to the steering wheel and traveled by the front half of the car while the rear half went into the parking area. I was very relieved to find that he was breathing, though shallowly.

The rookie came running over to me when I announced I had found the driver. As I began to look at the man and evaluate his condition, I turned to the rookie and told him,

"Hey, kid, keep looking, no one says this guy was the only one in the car."

It turns out he was, but we had to check. Recreating the scene, it appears that the car, traveling at a ridiculous rate of speed, had spun out. Halfway through spinning out, the car had impacted a large sign for the shopping area and split it right at the firewall. The rear half of the car tumbled into the parking area. The front half of the car, with the driver attached, continued forward another 60 or so yards. I later found the drive shaft for the vehicle over 80 yards away in a field. It is a very fortunate thing that this happened at about 3:30 in the morning. A couple of hours earlier and the bar that was in that shopping area would have been letting out, and dozens of people would have been in that parking lot. Had this happened at that time, it would've been a much higher body count. As it was there was only one person in the car, and he died later at the hospital. Later, tests showed his blood alcohol content at three times the legal limit.

Drunks Are Dangerous
(And Funny)

Arresting drunk drivers has always been a passion of mine. Not only because they are a grave danger to everyone on the road, including themselves, but because often times they are entertaining as hell. Their lies, excuses, and rants have provided my fellow officers and me with hours of laughter, not only immediately on the scene, but in the retelling of the story time and time again. There is something about a drunk who is too inebriated to understand how poorly they are conducting themselves that can be actually amusing to watch.

One of the best places to watch for drunk drivers are the main roads that lead into and out of the city, especially for the 20 minutes before and after the bars close. One morning, I was parked in a closed gas station lot, watching the main road that leads east out of the city. There was not much traffic that morning, and I was able to hear cars approach. I even have developed quite an ear for determining speed. On that road is a bridge, and that bridge has to sections of grate. The speed limit going over the bridge is 40 miles an hour. If a car is traveling at that speed, the sound of it going over the grate should be just about three seconds. If it is two seconds, it means that the car is going more than 50 mph; if it is one second, the car is doing better than 80 miles an hour. Seated in the parking lot (as I was) I was listening to the cars go over the bridge and timing the sound of them going over the grate.

Just as I was about to give up on this particular area and move on to a different location I heard a noise that I just could not identify. It was coming from just over the bridge, and as the bridge has a rise in the middle, I could not see what was approaching. The sound was akin to a freight train rumbling along. As the vehicle making the sound came into view, I found myself in an unusual position. Having over 20 years on the job at the time, I found myself stunned. The vehicle making the noise was an older model sedan, traveling over the bridge at about 40 miles an hour. The left front wheel was missing. The whole wheel was missing, not just the tire, but the rim as well. The brake rotor was dragging in the street, which was the cause of the great roar. As the metal dragged through the asphalt, a shower of sparks flew up under the car and behind it. So as this old car moved down the street, there was light and smoke show worthy of any '80's hair band.

As it passed me, I pulled out behind it and activated my lights and siren. After some distance, approximately a quarter mile, it finally stopped. Several young officers arrived to assist me. They arrived in such a timely manner that I had not yet approached the driver before I had two other cars with three offices total on the scene with me. I looked around and noted that some of the officers were quite young. I tried to determine which had the least experience and therefore would be the one I asked to assist, to make a learning experience for them as well. I chose Officer D, who had a few years' experience, but who I knew had little experience with drunk drivers.

I approached the driver and found a woman in her early 40s. It was evident at first look that when she had gone out that evening, she was probably very proud of her appearance. By

125

this time, however, her makeup was smeared, and her hair disheveled. Her blouse was partially un-tucked and buttoned askew. The stains on her clothing led me to believe that she had either drooled heavily or vomited on herself and had lost control of her bladder. Before I could even utter a word, she was already screaming at me. "Why are you pulling me over? I am doing nothing wrong. I am just a lady going home!" I made several attempts to speak to her and tell her why she was pulled over and to obtain her information, however, I could do nothing to stem the flood of ridiculous statements coming out of her mouth. "You are obviously a rookie, and a coward. You are a coward because instead of arresting drug dealers you choose to harass ladies who were going home and doing nothing wrong."

Eventually, in my frustration, I asked Officer D to obtain her information and to conduct the roadside sobriety tests. In the meantime, I used the cruiser's computer to run the information on the car and the car's owner. Looking at the driver's license picture of the car's owner, I determined that that the driver was the owner and I was able to run her information. In the meantime, I started writing out the citation, while keeping an eye on the roadside tests that were being conducted. I waited for Officer D to signal me his findings at the end of the test. However, there was no need. Casual observation of the tests as they were conducted told me that she had failed miserably. Throughout the examination, she continually asked why she had been pulled over in the first place, and speculated that it was because I was too afraid to deal with drug dealers. When it was pointed out to her that she was missing an entire wheel, she exclaimed. "So? What's the problem with that?! I only live a few miles away."

She was placed under arrest and transported to booking. In booking, she chose to take the breath test to determine her blood alcohol level. She failed that test as well, registering three times the legal limit. Throughout the booking process, she continued to allege that the rookie who had arrested her (indicating me) was nothing but a coward who likes to harass ladies. She also stated at one point that I had stolen her front left tire to justify stopping her for no reason. Like I said, drunks can be truly entertaining.

I like to be involved in drunken driving arrests even when I am not the officer who initiated the stop. I enjoy conducting the roadside sobriety tests and pride myself in being exceptionally thorough in my explanation and demonstration. The reports I write when I am the officer who administered the roadside sobriety tests have in the past-convinced defense attorneys to plead out the case. I am not bragging here. I have been approached by more than one defense attorney who has told me as much. One of my own idiosyncrasies when it comes to these tests is the 'signal' that I give to my fellow officers indicating that the subject has failed the test.

Often when you tell someone that they are under arrest, and they are drunk and not thinking correctly, that is the beginning of a fight or a foot chase. So I have developed a method that keeps them thinking that they are still safe while indicating to my fellow officers that they have failed and are to be arrested. I will say to the subject, "Now, you are not doing well, but I'm going to give you one more chance." I then ask the subject to put his two thumbs up as if to give a positive vote with both hands (or to imitate the 'Fonz' from *Happy Days*). I then ask them to touch their thumbs together. I show them how I want this by rotating my wrists and having my thumbs touch.

Usually, they will try this in imitation of me right in front. I will tell them that that was good. However, it is far too easy to do this in front where you can see, and I will ask them to do it again but behind their back. Thinking that they still have a chance to pass the test, they eagerly attempt what I requested. In doing so, they place their hands behind their back with their thumbs close together, making it easy for an officer standing there to grasp their thumbs and quickly apply handcuffs. I am confident that this little 'ruse' has prevented many a problem over the years. I have been proud to see that maneuver used by several other offices and I am told that it has spread to some surrounding towns as well.

One of the standard questions that we as officers will ask the driver we suspect of drunk driving is, 'How much have you had to drink tonight?' I can say with high confidence that the answer is 'two beers' or some variation; couple, one or two, etc. I don't know why this answer is so prevalent. I do know that having tested many of the people who told me this that it is a lie, as their blood alcohol content is far higher than two standard beers would produce. I have often asked these people where they bought these beers, because wherever it is they must serve some huge beers. I have only once found a man who told me the truth about what he had to drink that night. When I asked him, he went on a three-minute list of various types of alcohol and beer. He named not the only type of alcohol, but brand names and amounts as well. Given the rather impressive list that he gave me, I was stunned that he was able to tell me all this while standing. Hell, I was impressed that he could stand there all.

One morning, as I was driving around near a park, I could hear the sound of crashing nearby. After a brief search, I located a motor vehicle which was between two trees, one to the front of it and one to the rear. The driver was continually placing the car in drive and reverse and smashing into either of the two trees. I walked up to him and tapped on the window. This man was so incredibly inebriated that he refused to acknowledge that he was in a park, or that he was being stopped by the police. I had to reach into the thankfully open driver's window and shut the car off as it crashed from tree to tree. There is no safe way to do that, but I managed it. I pulled the driver out of the car and could tell by the way he struggled against me that there was no way I was going to be able to conduct roadside tests. I simply made my observations and took this gentleman to booking. At booking, this gentleman regained some of his composure and demanded that the booking sergeant let him go because he was arrested falsely. The booking sergeant asked him to relate what happened, and he told the following story.

"I was driving along the highway when this officer ran up to my car and knocked on the window. I continued driving because I know that he is a city officer and does not have the right to pull me over on the highway. The officer then jumped into my moving car and took my keys." To the credit of every officer in the room, no one broke into laughter. The booking video recorded every word. When I heard this case was going to go to trial, I begged the district attorney to play that video for the jury. When the defense attorney heard how eager I was to have the video played, he wanted to re-watch it before the trial started. It seemed that the first time he watched it, he only watched long enough to hear his client refuse to take any tests.

He had missed his client making these ridiculous claims. Very shortly after that a plea arrangement was reached.

You Cops

Whenever someone comes into the hospital with a gunshot wound, or a stab wound, or what appears to be the result of domestic violence, the hospital staff is required by law to contact the police. One morning, at just about daybreak, I was sent to the hospital to interview a male who had been brought in with a gunshot wound to the leg. I arrived on scene and was directed by the staff to a treatment room. Upon entering the room, I saw that the patient was a male of about 19 years old whom I had dealt with many times before.

This man had shown great contempt for police officers in the past. At his young age, he had been arrested multiple times, a few by me. He was well known as a burglar, drug dealer, and a gang member. Here I would like to interject my humble opinion about 'gangs' in my city. Like many things that happen in my city, sloth is almost always the downfall. Many projects are started or conceived only to be given half effort and rushed to a conclusion. The gangs in the city are no different. Let me state again that this is my opinion and by no means a verifiable fact. These groups who call themselves gangs would most likely be utterly destroyed, were they to venture into larger cities, and attempt to interact with the real hardened criminals that make up some of the street gangs in this country. I suppose it is fair to say I had about as much contempt for this man as he had for me. The difference

131

between the two of us was that he showed it openly, and I not, in an attempt to do my job.

I opened up my conversation by asking him to please tell me what it happened. His response was to look away from me, shrug, and suck air through his teeth. (God, how I hate that.) A brief conversation with the doctor informed me that the wound was likely from a rather high caliber round, and judging by the look, damage had been done at close range. I again spoke with the patient and asked what had happened. He shrugged again and replied, "I ain't got nothing to say to you." I went back and forth with this man several times. Each time, I received a similar response in his replies to me became more aggressive and less eloquent with each passing. Finally, I made a plea that I hoped would appeal to his desire to see me leave the room. I asked that if he was not going to tell me what had happened, he could at least say where it happened so that I might go to the location and establish a crime scene. He responded with venom in his voice, saying, "You're the cop; you figure it out." I turned and left the room, trying to figure how I was going to write the report with absolutely no information.

In the hallway as I was leaving the hospital, I was approached by a woman who walked up on me with such aggression that I actually believed I was about to be assaulted. She screamed, pointing her finger in my face, "You fucking cops never do anything! This is the third time my son has been shot, and you fucking cops never do anything!" I did not say a word to her. I knew I was incapable of speaking to her and maintaining my professionalism. I just gestured for her to follow me and I turned back to her son's room. As I entered the room, I motioned for her to stop just outside the door. She did as I instructed to my absolute amazement. Once inside the room, I addressed her son once again.

"I am one last time asking you to please tell me what happened or if you are still reluctant to tell me to at least give me a location so that I can begin my investigation."

He responded again. "You are the fucking cop; you fucking figure it out."

I turned to the mother and I hoped I hid my smug expression. To be honest, I probably failed in hiding it entirely. I told her that her estimation as to how much effort I put into this case was wrong. I told her that this exchange between her son and I had been repeated multiple times. I then asked since she was so knowledgeable as to how police should conduct themselves and what they should do in an instance such as this, how I should best proceed. I told her that given the one and only witness that I had to this case, her son, had early refused to give me any information whatsoever, I was rather stumped as for how to best proceed. I also made mention that perhaps having been shot three times, her son should consider some lifestyle changes. Her response to me was two words, and those words were not 'Happy Birthday.'

Rick Grimes Would Be so Disappointed in Me

There is an area of my city's downtown with their own no less than six bars within a two block radius. As you can well imagine, on a busy night, come closing time, the crowds in the street can get rather large. On one particular night, I was in that area as a precaution due to some rather large crowds. My attention was drawn to two young officers who were attempting to arrest a particular male whom they had caught dealing crack. He wasn't fighting them exactly; however, he was far from cooperative. As they struggled with him, I stood by, seeing no way that I could actively help, I watched their backs as they did their jobs.

From down the street, walking with a full head of steam, came a rather large woman. She was not tall, perhaps 5 foot four, but she weighed easily 230 pounds. The man being arrested was evidently her 'boo.' She charged at the two officers and attempted to pull one off of her man. I grabbed her and pulled her away, attempting to place her under arrest. I was having some difficulty getting her hands behind her back due to her 'stature.' As I ordered her to place her hands behind her back and attempted to make this happen, she yelled, "Let go of me, and I'll put my hands behind my back." Looking her over, I determined that if she were to place her own hands behind her back, the likelihood of struggle and injury was greatly

134

lessened. I then made the mistake of releasing her hand to allow her to place her own hands behind her back.

Like I said, this was a mistake because she promptly punched me in the face. I reached out and again took hold of her wrist to attempt to regain control, and to be honest not to be punched in the face again. At this point, this rather large woman opened her mouth and bit the back of my right hand, hard. Understand two things about the situation; first, we were surrounded by dozens upon dozens of onlookers who all seemed to actively support this woman and her crack-dealing boyfriend. Second, being a nerd, I have watched countless zombie based movies and television shows and I know that this is what 'patient zero' would look like. It crossed my mind for the briefest of moments given my vast knowledge of zombies and their methods, that I would be justified to shoot her in the head. I didn't, of course, I merely wrestled her back to control and cuffed her.

As I walked her to the cruiser so that I could transport her to booking, out came to the cell phones I saw no less than six persons shoving their cell phones, yelling to this woman that it was okay they got the whole thing on film, and the officer's brutality was being recorded. 'My brutality?' I had been as cooperative as possible with this violent woman. I'd given her the opportunity to cooperate with my hands off. For this, I was punched in the face and bitten. Despite her struggles and her leaning her mass to nearly pull us both to the ground, I managed to get her into the car and closed the door. I turned to face the crowd in the line of cell phones recording my actions. Using my flashlight, I illuminated the circular teeth pattern on the back of my right hand. Suddenly, I was alone. No one on the street any longer seemed to care about recording the incident. While I had struggled with the fat woman and it looked as though I were dragging her, every camera was pointed in my direction. But when my injury, a bite mark from a potential zombie was on display each camera found its way to its pocket.

I Read Books Too

The next town over from mine has a rather large campus for the local university. Every year, the months that schools in session show a significant uptick in calls for service in the downtown area. Every year, a flood of late teen to early 20's kids flood the downtown area of the city. They rent cheap apartments in groups of four or five. They throw parties where hundreds of guests arrive. They drink themselves to a near coma at the downtown bars. Mostly, or at least it seems like mostly to my mind, they go out of their way to explain how much smarter they are than I am.

One morning, I was dispatched to a corner in the downtown area. The notes of the call were that a male was laid out on the sidewalk. Now, 75% of the time calls like this are 'gone on arrival' calls. By the time the information has gone to channels, been given to me, and I get to the location, the drunk has gone home. That was not the case in this matter. As I arrived at the designated corner, I did, in fact, see a male lying on his back near the corner named in the call. He was well dressed, with a collared shirt and khakis. He probably looked rather nice when he set out that evening. Whatever events had led him to this corner, however, did nothing for his appearance as he was now quite disheveled.

Upon further inspection, I noted several things. First, a wet stain on the building indicated that the man had been urinating up against the building when he passed out. Second, there was a slight downhill angle to the sidewalk from the building to the street, causing the urine to flow to a puddle on the sidewalk. Third that the gentleman must have drunk an awful lot as there was a significant pool. Lastly, the gentleman had the unfortunate timing that caused him to pass out directly in that puddle. I called for medics to check him out and I put on some latex gloves because I just knew I would have to touch him. I approached and poked him in the shoulder.

"Get up, get up, get up," I said as I prodded his shoulder with a gloved index finger. I received only a noncommittal grown in response. I shook him a little more firmly and said, "Come on now, get up."

This time he responded with words saying, "Go away."

I continued to poke his shoulder, rocking his body and I now inquired, "Do you know that you're lying in a puddle of your own piss?"

His response came out mumbled but completely intelligible, "Do you know that I just fucked your mother?" He began to move, and by this time, I had conducted a more than cursory examination. I found no injuries and concluded that the worst thing that happened to him, so far, was that he had drunk far too much. As he was now conscious and not injured, there was no longer need for the medics, and I waved them off. I did this not to punish the young man, but to keep the ambulance available for persons who might truly need them. I stood my young, wet, suspect up, and handcuffed him. I was placing him under protective custody.

Protective custody is when someone is held due to their intoxication. It is not a criminal matter, and no charges are brought. They are simply held until they become sober enough to once again make good decisions. Here this man was obviously not making good decisions. It is not very smart to question the morality of someone's mother, especially if that someone has the ability to lock you away. (See, bad decisions.) I transported this man to booking and began the process. I obtained his information attempted to communicate to him the reasons everything happened tonight, check in for warrants and outstanding court matters. I wish I could say that it all went smoothly. It did not; as our young scholar began to wake up, he also became belligerent. I wish I could recall his exact phrasing, but to be honest, he was still very drunk, and his words were slurred, so my memories are not perfect. I do remember the intent of what he said.

This young man of 22 explained to me how he was much smarter than I was. He explained that he reads books. He said this in such a manner as to indicate that I either didn't or couldn't read books, not being as smart as him. Typically, I do not engage with drunks. You can't win an argument with someone who doesn't fathom what's being said. They just get loud and repeat themselves a lot. (Drunks actually do repeat themselves an awful lot.) This time I couldn't help but speak up. I had to shut him up somehow; booking was becoming impossible with his rants.

I walked over to where he sat cuffed to a bench. As I stood above him, I said in a stern but calm manner, "Look, I get it, you're 22 years old, and you've just realized how much there is to learn in this whole wide world. It is a very empowering feeling to have the world shown to you and understand how much knowledge there is to obtain. Right now, however, you are drunk and can not see how stupid you are being." I paused here to let him rile and rant about the word stupid, and when he was done, I continued. "I am 45 years old, in case the math is too much for you, that means I'm 23 years older than you. I had obtained my degree before you, learned to walk, and I've read far more books than you've had the opportunity to." I paused and watched his eyebrows wiggle as he tried to understand what I was saying and as he began to retort I interrupted and continued my own little rant. "You choose to call me stupid because you believe that since my job doesn't require a higher education that I didn't obtain one. You have overlooked however a few simple comparisons between you and I. Only one of us is going home at the end of today, and only one of us stinks of piss."

I finished the booking and turned the prisoner over to the transportation officer. Now here our brilliant and well-educated young man could've walked to the van, gone to his cell, slept a few hours, and gone home. He chose, however, to yank free of the transportation officer and attempt to flee on foot. This man, this genius, tried to run, while handcuffed out of a gated sally port surrounded by officers. So now instead of a nap, he found himself with criminal charges and a court date. Not to mention when the Dean of students for the college finds out about his activities he stands a good chance of being dismissed from school. Through all this, he continued to maintain his superiority to the dry, sober men who had to lift his piss-soaked body into the van for transportation.

As I said earlier, many times, the students will rent an apartment or a house in groups of four or five. They will then proceed to throw massive parties were hundreds like them will arrive. We as police officers have little interest in breaking up such a party. In fact, if we receive no noise complaints, we will often ignore the situation entirely. Well, that's not quite accurate; we will monitor from a distance, and stay close by to the area in case something goes wrong. Something often goes wrong. I have assisted in the ending of many of these parties, and it has become my habit to start counting bodies as they walk out. In one small two-bedroom cottage, I once had to give up counting when I reached 300 because that meant they were now 300 people milling about the street behind me. I shudder to think what would happen if a fire broke out in one of these severely overpacked parties.

Unless we have to, we try not to be overly aggressive when breaking up these parties. The last thing we want is a herd of drunken young people scattering and running through a suburban neighborhood. This doesn't mean that our calm approach doesn't often result in panicked and stupid behavior. On one instance, we were breaking up a party at a rented house on a corner lot. It was the third noise complaint since midnight, and they had already been warned. We knocked on the front door. We saw but pretended not to, the residents were peeking out the window. As more officers arrived, I began to walk around the house to get a visual through the windows of how large this party actually was. Around the corner, I observed that a good portion of the party had left via the back door and was now attempting to make their escape through a gate in a wooden fence that surrounded the property.

There were between 20 and 30 of them in the backyard. They could not figure how to open the gate to the fence. Two of what I assume were the leaders of the bunch had bent the corner of the gate and were attempting to help people climb through the V-shaped notch they had created. I walked up and as calmly as possible told them to back away from the gate. Once I had the area of the gate clear, I turned the handle push the gate into the yard. They were attempting to push open the pull open door. I looked them over, and they all stared at me wondering what the next move was.

I only asked one question. "Isn't your school an engineering school?" I then stepped away from the gate and allowed these 'geniuses' to go on their way.

Sergeant J and the Burning Car

Very early on in my career, as a matter of fact, it was before I was allowed to write alone, I reported to work for the second shift (4 to 12). On this shift worked Sergeant J. Sergeant J was a small woman in her early 50s. She was short, perhaps, 5 foot four or 5 foot five. I don't think she weighed 120 pounds even with her gear on. Her salt-and-pepper hair was cut short almost in the man's style, giving her an almost masculine appearance, overall. She was at the time one of the top three most senior sergeants in the department. It was well known that if Sergeant J liked you, you would be treated fairly; and as a rookie, evaluated fairly. There was a rumor that if she didn't like you she would make your life hell, and your evaluations would suffer. Over the years as I've grown to know, admire, and befriend Sergeant J, I have learned that those rumors were completely untrue. Despite any personal feelings she had for anyone, one way or the other she was always fair and professional in her job. As a rookie, I was terrified of her. As her friend, I'm still a little intimidated.

At the end of roll call, she called me over and explained a few things to me. She told me that my schedule partner for the evening would be running late due to some emergency at home. She explained that I would be riding alone for the beginning of the shift until my partner could come in. She handed me the keys and said a few things that scared the hell out of me.

"I am trusting you out there by yourself. If you make a mistake, and I find out that you didn't ask anybody first before acting, I will kill you. Do I make myself clear?"

Now under most circumstances 'I will kill you' is a figure of speech and certainly not meant to be taken literally. At the time however as a scared 20 something kid, I believed her wholeheartedly and I panicked, trying to get out of the station. "Yes, sir," I replied and I was greeted by an intense stare. I realized my mistake. After all those months in the Academy 'yes, sir simply shot out of my mouth. I quickly corrected with 'yes, ma'am.' The intense stare that had shot back at me at my first response somehow became more threatening and spoke of my imminent demise. She actually squared up on me in a quasi-rating stance. She took a deep breath which what I now imagine was a preparation for a thorough tongue-lashing. I imagined at the time that she was preparing to breathe fire on me. I grabbed the keys, turned on my heels, and quite literally ran from the station.

I quickly inspected the cruiser, jumped in the driver's seat, started the engine, and drove off. It was my intention to find a quiet spot out of the way and wait patiently for my partner. There was no way I was going to find any trouble, with which to incur Sergeant J's wrath. I did not get three blocks when I began to know a lack of power in the accelerator. The engine also did not sound right to me. I am not now nor was I then a car expert. I know when it sounds wrong, plus I certainly cannot diagnose any problem. I turned around and headed back to the station. I pulled the cruiser into its assigned parking area and went into the station. I found Sergeant J to report my problem. As I clumsily attempted to explain to her my feelings about the car and its performance, the look on her face was apparent to anyone who happened to be looking. I am absolutely sure that what was running through her mind was that the stupid rookie is scared and afraid to go out by himself.

She huffed, or perhaps it was more over harrumph and stormed out of the station to inspect the car. I followed closely, but not so close to be in striking distance should she turned around. By the time we had returned to the cruiser, thick smoke and flames were coming out from under the hood. I remember standing there, watching this thick smoke roll into a clear blue sky and thinking that this would be a defining moment in my relationship with Sergeant J. She would always remember me as the dumb rookie who burnt up a cruiser. Like I said before, I'm not a car guy. I can't tell you what caused this or even what could have caused this, all I know is the car wasn't acting properly; and after I had returned it to the station, it was on fire. We opened the hood and several fire extinguishers later, the fire was put down. There was a fire station within view of this whole spectacle and 20 minutes later, they showed up in their big, red, shiny truck and put a couple hundred gallons of water on the car too. They also cut the battery cables and pulled a couple other wires that I couldn't identify out as well. Those firefighters really do love destroying stuff.

Many years later, Sergeant J has become my friend. We have enjoyed many conversations about our similar interests. She and I are both firearms instructors, as well as defensive tactics instructors, and we have shared techniques on those subjects. We've also engaged in the standard cop practice of telling 'war stories.' One day, I related this story to her. The details of that day were still fresh in my mind 20 plus years later. It had been a very traumatic moment for me. Sergeant J told me that I must have an excellent memory because she did

145

not recall it at all. To her was just another thing that went wrong, another thing to fix. It was not such a traumatic moment for her. It was just another day, and it did not sit in her memory the way it sat mine.

You Never Forget Your First Time

The very first time that I made a 'solo' arrest, an arrest where I was not assisted in any way by a senior officer, was at a bar that was and is infamous. This bar has gone by at least a half-dozen names since I have been involved with the department. During my time as a dispatcher, I had sent many officers to this location for a variety of reasons. I had, up until this night, never actually been inside this bar. As a matter of fact, I had never really been inside any bar. Bars and clubs were never my scene and I do not find myself comfortable in that environment. That may be because of the job, which is taught me that these places are far too often the scene of trouble.

This particular establishment is in the middle of downtown. It is directly across the street from a bus terminal, and on the main street leading through the downtown area. It is mainly a Cape Verdean bar. This is not due to any written rule or established guideline. It is just a matter of fact that the employees, owners, and clientele of this bar have always been, primarily, Cape Verdean. On this night, I was working alone, that is to say in a one-man car for one of the very first times. In addition, I was also assigned as an early car. If I haven't already explained an *'early'* car comes in one half hour before the shift and does not attend roll call to avoid a gap in coverage.

I was dispatched to this bar, and the notes of the call were that there was a male refusing to pay for his drinks.

I parked out front, exited my cruiser, put my hat on, and walked inside. It was dark inside, but my eyes adjusted quickly. I noted that there was a large circular bar dominating the room, with the jukebox and pool table in the corners. There were about 30 people in the bar including myself and the bartender. A quick glance around the room showed me that there were only two Caucasians in the establishment. I was one of them. I approached the bartender, as she gestured to the other Caucasian in the room as the cause of the problem. Seated at the bar, where the bartender had gestured, was a white male of about 30. He was dressed rather shabbily in dirty jeans and a red T-shirt. He had long hair which was in no way combed more orderly. It also appeared that he had not washed that hair in some time.

Being a rookie and up until that point not having been the one required to do the talking at most calls, I did what I thought I should do. Bear in mind that most of what I knew about how police officers speak had gone from television. Perhaps, I should've paid a little more attention to my senior officers. Having been the dispatcher and clerk before the Academy, my bosses had seen it fit to give me a lot of clerical work after I graduated the Academy. I had a frighteningly small amount of street experience because of this. Putting on the bravest and sternest face I could, I approach this male placed my hands on my hips and what I hoped was an authoritative stance. I now recognize that this is the stance a person takes they don't know what else to do. "What seems to be the problem here?" I asked, the longhaired guy was refusing to pay for his drinks.

"The problem is all the freaking nachos in here," he responded in an all too clear and loud voice. Only he didn't

148

say, 'nachos,' he said another word that began with an 'N.' This initially set me back on my heels as I certainly wasn't expecting that response. A quick glance around the room told me that I was not mistaken, and he had said the word that I thought he had. At this point, several gentlemen seated nearby stood up and politely offered to handle the situation for me. Well, they weren't exactly polite, and they weren't actually proposing to help me. What they did offer certainly wouldn't have ended the situation involving the unpaid for drinks, but it would've presented me with an entirely new set of problems.

I determined that were I ever to have any respect out on the street I needed to handle the situation and take care of it quickly. I also decided that if I did not get this longhaired idiot out of here, he was going to catch one hell of a beating. I quickly grabbed a fistful of that hair. It was, in fact, disgusting and greasy. I wrapped it around my fist, grabbed his arm with my other hand, and rushed him out of the bar. On the way out, I opened the door with his head. This had the desired effect of calming the patrons of the bar. Upon seeing me handle the man in this way, they were less inclined to become personally involved. I got the male outside and attempted to place him in handcuffs. I could not understand why I was having such difficulty with this. He was drunk, and I was well-trained. This should have been a two-second job. It was tough, however. He knew each move that I was going to make and how to slip out of it. I finally managed to get them cuffed and back to the station for booking. It was there I learned why he was so good at slipping away from my grip.

It seems this man had been a police officer with another agency in the recent past. He had however been dismissed from that position. The rumor was he had been dismissed from that position for multiple 'excessive force' cases. I was never able to dispute or confirm that. The sergeant that evening pulled me aside and asked me if I were willing to place this man under protective custody rather than arrest him. He asked me to do this because the man had been a police officer and as a courtesy to someone who had done the job. Whether or not I agreed with this, I certainly was not going to argue with the sergeant on my second week on the job. I agreed to this and walked down to the cell with the sergeant, so he could explain to the man what was happening.

The cell door was opened, and the sergeant explained to him that he would be placed under protective custody rather than arrested. As a former police officer, I'm sure this man understood what the sergeant was saying completely. I also, in the next few moments, realized why this man was no longer a police officer. As the sergeant was almost complete in his explanation, the man in the cell spat forth an impressive amount of saliva and phlegm, striking with sergeant directly in the forehead. He then kicked the sergeant in the groin. I shoved the man and slammed the door shut. Now, the gentleman was not a PC but was under arrest and had new charges to go with it.

In this book, it has been my practice not to name anyone. I do not name any businesses, fellow officers, or even family members. I do this for anonymity sake. I will mention that I do remember this man's name. Thirty years later, I have no problem recalling his name. I guess it's true you never forget your first time.

Good Thing We Aren't in Kansas Anymore

In July 2006, my brother and I decided to take a vacation together. We rented a car and over a two-week period drove cross-country and back again. We had no agenda and only vague destinations in mind. We took a rather circuitous route that brought us through 31 states. It is while we were traveling through Kansas that this next story takes place. It does not sound like a police story right now, but it will be by the end.

It was a Sunday as we made our way through Kansas. We were off the main highway because we had taken a side venture to see the largest ball of twine and the geographical center of the United States. The largest ball of twine seems like a very cliché thing to do. That is exactly why we did it. The geographical center of the United States was not very far from the ball of twine, and it seemed like a cool thing to see. Do you know what is next to the geographical center of the United States? Absolutely nothing, it is in the middle of a vast field along a very long secondary road, and there was nothing to see for miles. Well, I did see a cow. Returning back from this side venture, we were moving along a highway that had a very set pattern to it. There were long stretches where the speed limit was 65 miles an hour, and every 10 miles or so a small group of buildings, barely a strip mall would pop up, and the speed limit would drop to 35 mph. I was driving at the time, and it was about midday. We had not seen another car for about an hour and a half. This is not an exaggeration, we had actually commented on it just before the focal point of the story.

While entering one of these areas of 35 miles an hour, I saw the police cruiser in a parking lot. I was not worried. I had slowed down. I had actually gotten the rhythm down, or at least I thought. As we passed the cruiser, he pulled out of the lot and put his lights on behind us. I immediately pulled over. I guessed that he had a call and I got out of his way as efficiently as I could. He did not have a call he was pulling me over. That's fine. He's doing his job. I looked to my right and saw that my brother was fishing through the glove compartment for the vehicle's registration. I told him to stop; he looked at me frustrated and asked why. I explained to him that this officer had no idea what he was walking up on and seeing a guy search for something during a traffic stop is a warning sign to officers. I rolled down the window and kept my hands on the steering wheel and waited for the officer to approach. He approached and informed me that he had clocked to me going 37 in a 20-mile an hour zone. I apologized and explained that I had not seen a 20-mile an hour sign. I then handed him my license and instructed my brother to get the registration. I took that moment to identify myself as a police officer and showed him my badge and identification. He took the license and registration and said, "Yup they give me tickets too."

He was an older gentleman probably in his early 50s and had probably been on the job for quite some time. He had that sort of ease about him that I have learned to recognize in senior officers. He returned and asked me why the plates on my car were from a different state than my driver's license. I explained to him that it was a rental car, and sometimes they have cars from all over on their lots. He told me he'd never heard of that and went back to his cruiser. He returned a few minutes later and handed me a citation which totaled $165. He informed me that I could appear in a particular courthouse in two weeks' time to fight the citation if I so chose. I looked at him and shrugged. He got back in his cruiser and drove off. I was determined not to let this one ruin my day, or my trip. No rule says police officers don't get tickets. If I am doing something wrong, I expect to be called on it. I am not above the law, and in fact, I should be constantly vigilant. In theory, I know the law better than most and therefore have no excuse. However, it is a well-known practice, that for minor violations, a 'professional courtesy' is extended to brother and sister officers. I never expect this, and it has always been my practice to hand out a warning whenever feasible to her brother officer.

My brother and I finished our vacation, we saw Vegas, the Hoover Dam, the Grand Canyon, Hollywood, Mount Rushmore, and much more. It was a wonderful trip, and I hope someday to do it again. The ticket was an inconvenience but not one that marred the entire excursion. Once I got home, I paid the ticket online, and once I had my confirmation that it had been paid I decided to handle my frustration in my usual manner. I was a smartass. I looked up the Sheriff's Department that employed the gentleman who gave me the citation. I found the actual Sheriff's name and his office address. I then sent the following letter:

'Dear Sheriff;

I hope this letter finds you well. I was concerned to see that your county and department are in a desperate financial situation. As a 20-year veteran of law enforcement, I can think of no other reason that your officers (deputies) would see fit to hand out a citation to his brother officer on a Sunday morning when no other vehicles were in sight, and a minor infraction had occurred. I admit that if in fact there was a 20-mile an hour zone, I was, in fact, doing more than 25 miles an hour. I did not see a 20-mile an hour sign and I am not disputing its existence. If your county and department needs money so badly that these tactics are in order, you have my heartfelt sympathy. Enclosed with this letter please find a $10 bill and a coupon for Subway. It is my hope that today at least you will have a decent lunch.

Fraternally;

A Brother Officer'

Parking Tickets

As a police officer, you are called upon to intrude in people's lives in a variety of ways. Traffic stops encounters on the street and calls for disturbances all require police to interact with individuals in the course of their lives. Truth be told, in most cases, these encounters prompt very little in the way of reaction from the general population. Sure, people get angry at a traffic stop or finding police knocking on the door, but in my experience, I have never seen anyone get quite as upset as a person who just received a parking ticket. Parking tickets account for nearly half of the calls for complaint at the station. I personally have been met with some of the most volatile tirades from people who have just received a parking violation.

It has always been my practice that if I am going to write a parking citation, I will cite every car in the immediate area that is in violation. One morning while I was citing a few cars along one particular street, I was met by a gentleman who was exceptionally irate. He approached me with so much anger that I actually prepared myself for a physical assault. He had in his hand the green slip that indicated he had found one of my parking tickets.

"You ticketed my son's car!" he bellowed.

"It's entirely possible; I have ticketed quite a few cars today," I replied as matter-of-factly as possible.

"You cited him for parking more than six inches from the curb," he yelled, shoving the citation less than six inches from my face.

"Yes, I probably did. I wrote a few tickets for that offense this morning," I replied as I continued to write another ticket for another car for the exact same offense.

"Well, I measured it, and it was ten inches from the curb," he stated rather smugly.

"Yes sir," came my reply as calmly as I could muster, "which would, in fact, be more than six inches."

I'm not sure what made him angrier, the fact that I pointed out the obvious or the admittedly condescending manner in which I did it. Regardless, it did nothing to calm him, and he again shoved the citation at my face.

"I want you to write ten inches on this ticket," he demanded.

"Okay, sir," I responded, "however, I have to say that if you plan to use as a defense for a ticket for parking more than six inches from the curb the fact that you were parked more than six inches from the curb, you will probably lose the appeal."

I wrote ten inches in the margin of the ticket next to the offense and handed it back. The man took it and looked at me with a smug look on his face as if to say, "There, I beat you." I turned and walked away, ticketing another car as I did. The stream of insults and vulgarities that came out of that man's mouth was completely uncalled for. He doesn't even know my mother.

As a patrolman assigned to a particular patrol area, I have been called on from time to time to attend community meetings. I recall one such meeting in which the entire hour was taken up with complaints regarding illegally parked cars. I remember being rather proud of this because to my mind it meant that I had reduced crime in the area to such a level that this was now the primary concern. I took this information with me the next night I went on patrol. I tagged over two dozen cars on that shift. One such ticket that I wrote was for a trailer parked on the street not attached to a motor vehicle. Not long after sunrise. I was dispatched to that area to meet a complainant regarding a parking ticket. The woman who owned the trailer was beside herself with anger. I don't remember all the names she called me, but I do recall 'idiot' being among them. She informed me that her cousin is a state police officer. She further told me that her cousin had said that there was no violation and that I had no right to issue that ticket. Having been accused of being an idiot, I attempted to form my reply as intelligently as possible. It probably came out sarcastic.

"Well, ma'am, as the state police primarily patrols highways, and as very little parking is done on highways, I'm going to go ahead and assume that your cousin is not an expert in this matter. You are more than welcome to bring your cousin to the appeal, where I will gladly show him the city ordinance that gives me the justification for this ticket."

I offer a word of warning to all those reading this. In my city as well as many cities in the area, there is a law that makes it illegal, and arrestable, to destroy a parking violation. I am not aware of one for moving violations, but I know that one exists for tearing up a parking violation. This law has been the cause of many stunned faces. Angry people, thinking that they were getting the better of me by tearing up the ticket as a form of protest have found themselves facing criminal charges in addition to the $10 fine. I'm not going to lie; cuffing some of these belligerent folk has given me a quiet pleasure.

Trick or Treat

Halloween has always been one of my favorite days of the year. As a little boy, I always dressed as Batman. I always wanted to be Batman and I think I got about as close as I could. Let's think about it for a moment; Batman wears dark clothing, goes out at night, he has a cool car, and a belt full of cool shit. Batman catches criminals. I go out at night; my shift is from midnight to eight. My uniform is dark, midnight blue. The police cruiser was a pretty cool car. I have a belt full of cool shit. I catch criminals. So I have Halloween all the time. As a matter of fact, my very first day in the Academy was Halloween.

As a police officer, Halloween often presents some truly amazing sights. I remember on one particular night being sent to a bar fight. When I got to the bar, I found a young man seated on the sidewalk, holding his head. When I got closer, I noticed he was holding a towel to his head, and that towel was soaked through with blood. It is important to note here that the man was dressed as Spiderman. I found his mask later inside the bar. It was a pretty good costume, rather authentic. He probably paid quite a bit of money for it. I hope it wasn't a rental because it was ruined with blood. I called for the medics, broke out the first aid kit, and began to bandage the man while I asked him what happened. He explained that he was talking to a girl, and evidently, there was another guy there, who felt that nobody else should be talking to her. A fight ensued, and the other guy hit Spidey with a barstool. I asked him if he could describe the other guy. He said that he knew the guy from school, that his name was Steve, and that he was dressed as Captain America.

(As a cool sort of a side note, in the comics, Captain America s secret identity is Stephen Rogers.)

The story actually upset me. First, because I always thought that Spiderman and Captain America were buddies. To let a woman come between them is unthinkable. Second, and to my nerd mind perhaps, more importantly, Captain America hit Spidey with a stool? Really, a barstool? If, and I do mean if, I have to accept Captain America beating Spiderman with anything, it has to be his shield. A somber day followed as I had to lock up two of my favorite superheroes when they ran into each other again and began to fight again. Once I saw him, I was rather disappointed in Captain America. The costume was poorly put together, and his physique told me that it was most likely that the super soldier serum had begun to wear off.

At that same bar, one-year prior, I was called to what was described as a large fight in the back parking lot. When I arrived, I found four women actively fighting. I mean truly fighting, fists and elbows flew. Hair was pulled. And clothing was torn. This was a four-way match. I could discern no teams. The participants were: Snow White, Princess Jasmine, Cinderella, and the Naughty Secretary. I have to admit I really didn't want to break it up. It was quite a show. I know you have some questions and I will do my best to answer them. Honestly, I think the secretary was winning the fight. Yes, I saw boobs, Jasmine's were the nicest. No, I didn't frisk them, as there was no place in any of their costumes where they could have secreted a weapon. In the secretary's case, her costume barely contained the gifts God gave her, she would never have been able to hide anything else.

What a World

Sometimes, imagination can be an essential and powerful tool. I remember one night, it was summer, and probably about 3 A.M. I was working alone, but my friend Officer T had a young rookie with him. By young, I mean this young man had been less than a week on the job. I heard dispatch send them on a call regarding threats. As I was close by, I decided to stop by and assist if I could.

We arrived at almost the same time, and the three of us approached the house together. We knocked, and an elderly woman in a housecoat ushered us quickly inside. It was a small house, and I remember thinking she has far too much furniture for the small rooms, as everywhere we stood seemed crowded. I stepped back to allow Officer T, and the young rookie to handle the call. It is important to have the rookies conduct as many interviews as possible, as speaking to people and taking notes are a huge percentage of the job. The meeting went something like this;

Rookie: So, ma'am, who is threatening you?

Woman: She lives in the North End.

Rookie Was she here, when she threatened you? Or did she call you?

Woman: I can hear her when I sipped my coffee. I can hear her say she's going to kill me.

The young rookie turned to Officer T and me, with a desperate look on his face that showed he had 1000 questions for us. But sometimes there are no simple answers, Officer T merely gestured for him to continue. Officer T, as well as I, wanted to see how this progressed without our interference.

Rookie: Well, ma'am, what kind of car does she drive so that we can look for her as she travels?

Woman: Oh, she doesn't drive.

Rookie: Well, if she doesn't drive, how will she get here to hurt you?

Woman: Oh, she doesn't have come here to kill me. She is a witch.

The stunned look on the rookie's face made holding back our laughter almost impossible. I remember Officer T turning and biting on a knuckle. This, of course, did nothing to relieve the tension that poor young rookie felt. I had a moment of inspiration and I stepped forward, speaking for the first time.

"Well, ma'am, tonight is your lucky night, you see I am the first born son of the last living Ojibwa shaman and I can help you." I pulled out my notepad sat down at the table and very cautiously drew out a set of symbols. I don't recall exactly what symbols I wrote. I had recently read a book about Norse mythology and I believe I used some Runes I had seen in that book. After writing down about four symbols, I made a great show of very carefully folding the paper. I folded the paper down into one of those small triangles kids use in school to pass notes. I turned to the woman and spoke as though I were imparting secret knowledge.

"This charm is a potent spell, specifically against witches. You must never unfold it, you must never take it outside, and above all never get it wet." I remember that last bit was because I had recently seen the movie gremlins.

The woman took it from me almost reverently saying, "I will put it in my Bible."

"That is just perfect," I replied, and the three of us turned to leave. Officer T turned to his young rookie and instructed him that he had just learned a valuable lesson regarding dealing with people and saying what needed to be said to make them feel safe and happy. That woman never did call the police regarding threats from which again. By the way, I checked, she lived for many years afterward and died of natural causes in a hospital.

The Plan

One warm midweek day in early summer, I took a detail directing traffic. This is always a risky venture. You never know if you will end up on a quiet side street, or some six-way intersection in the heart of rush hour. On this particular day, I believed myself to be very lucky. The weather was warm, the breeze was light, the New England summer was not yet so hot, and a short-sleeved uniformed shirt was all that was required. No bulky jackets, no cumbersome gloves, no need to apply sunscreen to my pasty white skin on an hourly basis.

I was one block down a side street from a major thoroughfare. Behind me, the road had been dug up for the work on water main. This was easily the deepest hole I had ever seen on a city street. I do not exaggerate when I say it was at least 15 feet deep, 10 feet across, and stretching from sidewalk to sidewalk. All that material that had been in the hole (dirt and rocks) was piled up on the opposite side of the hole from me. So there, I stood in the street, behind me a canyon and a mountain. In front of me, I had two large orange sawhorses, two orange barrels with little blinking lights on them, and a 5 ft.^{2} sign also orange with the words '**road closed**.' A simple, but I felt, compelling message. I remember thinking to myself that I had fallen just right on this one. This was going to be easy money.

On occasion, maybe one car per hour would venture down my way. Most would figure out from the ample clues what to do all on their own and either turn right or left. Some of the drivers would be struck with indecision because, again, the steering wheel and the color orange make people stupid. To them, I would just point left or right, sometimes together sometimes individually, sometimes crossing my arms like the scarecrow in *The Wizard of Oz*. Once or twice I even jerked my thumbs to the side in a poor imitation of a 1960s go-go dancer. In short, I was enjoying a sunny day and easy money.

Then, along came a gray older Mercedes. It was driven by a woman who was also gray and definitely older. I do not know if her name was Mercedes, probably not. As she drove up to my sign and barrels and looked impatiently at me, I smiled and pointed left and right. She did not smile and pointed forward. I shook my head I pointed to the '**road closed**' sign and again pointed left and right. She again pointed forward indicating that she wished to go straight down the street with the aforementioned mountain and canyon. I stepped to the side, I pointed at the impedance, I pointed again at my sign, and I again pointed left and right. By this time, I had also lost my smile. She responded by blowing her horn and pointing vigorously forward.

I shrugged. I moved one of the horses. I moved one of the barrels with its blinking light. I moved my no-nonsense '**road closed**' sign. And I waved her through. I had not left her a lot of room, so she drove slowly forward, and I walked alongside the car. As she approached the gaping canyon, she came to a stop and rolled down her window.

"What am I supposed to do now?!" she exclaimed, oddly exasperated. I too at this point had lost my patience. However, I had not lost my ability to be a smartass.

"Lady, I have no idea. Back there I told you to go left or right around the block. You insisted upon going straight. I figured you had a plan. And frankly, I was excited to see it."

I have since come to understand that everyone, well mostly everyone, feels that they are somehow special and more important than the average person. They are all for the rules, as long as those standards don't interrupt their plans. They will have every excuse in the book why that particular rule should not apply to them. They never think why that rule is there. In the above story, it was simply road construction that shut down the street that day. In many instances, however, the motorist does not know why that road is closed. It could be construction; it could be a gas leak. It might be a crime scene, a dangerous animal, an active gunfight, or some lunatic holding a child hostage. They don't know, and they don't care. All they know is they can't go down the street they want to go down.

So a message to all of you who someday soon will come upon a young officer standing behind a road closed sign. Sir or ma'am, that road is closed, even if you live 'right there.' You work 'right there.' You 'always go this way.' You 'just went that way this morning.' Your babysitter, grandmother, sister, mother, lover, godson, puppy, probation officer, best friend, or the guy you owe ten bucks, is waiting. The road is closed, find another way.

Talking to the Police

What follows are my answers to the most common questions and statements made to police officers. Actually, I can't speak for all police officers, only for myself. If you talk to most police officers, however, I believe that they will identify with at least 75% of my statements here.

- No, I have never shot anyone.
- No, I do not know your cousin who is a cop 80 miles away.
- Yes, it is, in fact, a real gun.
- No, I will not take out my gun to show it to you.
- No, I have never used my cuffs in the bedroom.
- No, I will not arrest your child for being bad. (And please stop threatening them with that. I do not want children afraid to approach me.)
- No, we do not get free doughnuts.
- Yes, I have indeed seen some crazy things.
- No, I will not arrest you so that you can leave work early.
- I am not sure if officer so-and-so is working. Also, I am not impressed that you know officer so-and-so.

While on the subject of ridiculous things said to and asked of police officers, there are a few jokes that civilians tell that stopped being funny around day two out of the Academy. When you notice a policeman walked into the room, and you shout, "I didn't do it!" or the variation where you point your friend and say, "He's right here, take him away!" You may think that you are funny and terribly original. However, I can virtually guarantee that every officer has heard that joke over 100 times in their first six months of service. In addition to this, the donut jokes are actually kind of old. (One might even say stale.)

When the officer first comes on the job, he or she is more than likely going to be assigned to the midnight shift. One of the very few things that are open on the midnight shifts our coffee/doughnut shops. I would challenge anyone who has to drive around for eight hours from midnight to eight to do so without getting a coffee or some related beverage. In addition to this, when an officer is set loose in a cruiser, he or she suddenly finds themselves rather alone. The coffee shop is a haven where they are likely to run into someone else, another officer, during their coffee. Suddenly, there is someone to talk to who is not complaining, nor a potential threat. So, sure, you will occasionally see a cruiser or multiple cruisers at or near a donut shop. But the reasons are far more complicated than just a chocolate glazed.

I tell all my friends and family that they only get one. What I mean by that is they are allowed one doughnut joke. One per lifetime. I'm amazed how many people when informed of that rule find it necessary to use their one that day. Sometimes, they are compelled to use it within the hour. I have one terrific friend named Bob. I have known Bob for, the better part, 15 years. Bob has never used his doughnut joke. I anticipate that he will either come up with a fantastic, original, and well-timed joke. It will either be that, or it will be part of my eulogy.

The Chair Shot

I have always been a fan of professional wrestling; it was one of the few things that my brother and I shared throughout our lives. This may seem, at this point, to be a random statement. I will, however, bring it into play shortly.

One day, close to 7 A.M., I was dispatched along with two young rookie offices to a potential domestic violence call. (Please bear in mind that our shift ends at 8 A.M.) The notes of the call were that a male had barricaded himself inside his apartment. In addition to this, he had assaulted his roommate with a 2x4 and the roommate believed his arm was broken. We arrived at the call which was a large apartment building up on the seventh floor. Large apartment building being a relative term. Large for my city is 11 floors, and 400 apartments in total. I also knew that this building was occupied entirely by the elderly, and special needs persons, such as the physically disabled, and those with psychological, and emotional disabilities. The Fire Department and ambulance were on scene, and all attempts to make contact through the door had failed. I had requested a street sergeant, who had promised me he was on his way (never got there). In a hallway full of emergency response personnel, everyone looked to me for a solution.

Listening at the door, I could hear a male voice calling for help. I instructed the firefighters to give me the key so that I could open the door to the apartment. I had everyone, except the rookies, step back and I opened the door. Upon opening the door, I saw there was a short hallway leading into the apartment at the end of that corridor a table had been pushed up to the entrance way. This meant that were we to enter the apartment we would have three choices. First: crawl under the table, second: jump over the table, third: shove the table aside. Complicating this matter was the fact that a man was standing just opposite us on the table holding a 2x4. His speech was accented and difficult to understand. However, I did hear quite clearly, "If you come in, I'll hit you." He looked like a Latino Martin Short, dressed in sweatpants and a white T-shirt. Honestly, he would not have been intimidating at all, were he not holding the 2x4. I needed a plan, I wanted a plan, and it dawned on me that it was my job to come up with a plan. I made a plan.

I looked over my two rookies. The first was built like a linebacker, tall, powerful, muscular, and evidently quite eager. The second was a young man whom I knew quite well and trusted. He did, however, look terrified. So here's the plan I came up with:

I pulled out my pepper spray and instructed the rookies as to what I wanted to happen. I would spray the suspect, causing a distraction. The young football player looking rookie would rush forward under the distraction and upend the table, forming a wall between the crazy man with the 2x4 and us. We would then use the table to push him up against the wall pinning him securing him, and we would follow up from there. The younger rookie would come with us in with his baton prepared in case things fell apart. This was a good plan. Like all good plans, it was dependent on things going perfectly. They did not.

I sprayed the suspect from the maximum distance my pepper spray would allow, I was very proud to see that I covered his face on the first shot and it seemed to be working. He did not drop the 2x4, but he blinked his eyes and leaned forward. And I gave the order, "Go!" The young pile of muscles wrapped in a rookie's uniform rushed forward, and his athleticism betrayed him. He flipped the table with such vigor that it completely upended, landing with its surface on the floor and four legs sticking up in the air. Because there was a hitch so early on in the plan, my athletic rookie paused. This caused him to become off-balance. The scared young rookie and I did not pause, and we three bounced into the room, *Three Stooges* style. I saw the athletic rookie bent forward. I saw the suspect raise the 2x4 above his head in a manner which led me to believe he was about to strike. At that moment, 20 years of watching professional wrestling finally paid off.

I hit him with the chair.

One Brave Little Boy

One morning, a little after sunrise, Officer S and I were assisting another officer at a traffic stop. It was a weekday morning and overcast. There wasn't a lot happening in the radio was unusually quiet. While Officer S and I watched over the officer at his traffic stop, the radio silence was broken by the voice of an unnerved dispatcher. We listen to these dispatchers all night long. We know the sounds of their voice when they're aggravated, when they're bored, and when they're scared. This one was scared.

The call was for a different section of the city than the one we were assigned to. The call was for a house fire. The call notes had indicated that a small child had escaped the house and run to a neighbor to call 911. According to the call notes, the child had told the dispatcher that they were still people inside the home. Officer S and I jumped into our cruisers. We turned on our blue lights and sirens, something rarely done on the midnight shift. We drove with all haste to the scene of the fire.

Upon arrival, we noted a few other officers were already there. We saw the house, and we saw that the house was billowing black smoke from everywhere. One of the officers on scene wiping sweat and tears from his eyes said, "We tried, the smoke is just too thick." I have a very distinct recollection of that moment. Officer S and I locked eyes from about 5 feet away.

Without vocalizing a word, we both said to each other, "I'll go if you go." We ran inside the house. On the first floor, the house had a rather open floor plan, and we were able rather quickly clear the area. I began to make my way up the stairs, and Officer S started soaking towels in the kitchen sink. He was behind me in seconds with a wet towel to breathe through and protect our head and ears.

When I reached the top of the stairs, the smoke was very thick, but I caught a glimpse of someone lying on their back in the bathroom. I yelled back that I had found something. I reached forward and grabbed an ankle and dragged that person to me. I am a pretty strong guy and with adrenaline even stronger. Officer S is by far stronger than me. I handed the person back to him, and he took what we later learned was a woman, from me with great ease and handed her to two other officers who had followed us in. I made my way into the upper hallway. In the bedroom, I could see another person, the second person that the call notes had indicated was in the house.

I made three attempts to get into that bedroom and pull that man out. I was not able to do it. The door frame was on fire, the smoke was getting thicker, and the floor was hot to the touch. I yelled back to Officer S what I saw and that I could not get into the room. We switched places so that I could get out of the smoke and he could make an effort in getting into the room. He came up with a plan that, at the time, seemed perfectly reasonable. He was going to reach into the room and grab the man by an arm and leg. I was then going to grab Officer S's feet and drag them both out. Like I said, at the time it seemed like a perfectly reasonable idea. We were both, however, suffering from smoke inhalation and probably not thinking perfectly clear. What his plan was asking me to do was to drag the 200-pound man lying unconscious in the room along with Officer S, who along with his equipment probably weighs in the neighborhood of 240 pounds. I remember being willing to try. I remember believing I could do it. In retrospect, I am glad we never tried.

About this time, the firefighters arrived. One of them came inside, and once he was suited up all his call out gear, he went inside and retrieved the man in the bedroom. Neither the woman we rescued from the bathroom nor the man from the bedroom was breathing when we got them outside. Other officers on scene, as well as EMS crews, were able to restore breathing and transport them to the hospital. Both suffered burns and smoke inhalation, but neither died.

I do not claim to be a brave man, nor do I pretend to be a better officer than any of my fellows. I will say that I am rather proud of my actions that day, along with the actions of the other officers on scene. Because we acted, because we acted as a team, because we acted without hesitation, those two people are still alive. The real hero that day is, of course, the young boy. He knew what to do, and he did it without hesitation. I've known grown men who are not capable of calling the police and giving pertinent information in an intelligible manner when under stress. This young boy not only escape the flames and thick black smoke that incapacitated two adults, but he found his way to a phone, called 911, and got help there quickly.

(When I grow up, I want to be just like him.)

Several months later, the emergency responders, police, fire, and EMS were invited to City Hall where we were acknowledged by the mayor and the City Council for our actions. I'm not generally comfortable in situations like this. I do, however, like to see my fellow officers and emergency responders recognized for their actions and bravery. I was rather proud to be able to bring my wife to this event. We were newly married, and she enjoyed watching the ceremony. I was also able to introduce her to many of the people that I work with. She took the award and hung it in our living room. I would never have done that, but secretly I do look at it from time to time with pride.

Finger off the Trigger

I have been fortunate in that I took to firearm skills rather quickly. I never had any trouble qualifying and I have consistently been in the upper 5% of my department for firearm scores. My interest in the area has led me over the years to a variety of duties involving firearms. My favorite among these has been that of an instructor. The portion of that job, which I found most thrilling, and most satisfying, has been helping shooters who are having difficulty qualifying. When a recruit is having trouble in the Academy qualifying with his or her firearm, they are sent back to the department on a Saturday to obtain remedial training. After this training, the recruit is given one last chance to qualify at the Academy, or fail. I have been used as the remedial instructor on several occasions and I am proud to say I have never lost the student.

I have, at times, been an instructor within the Academy setting. Although it may seem similar, this is entirely different from working with seasoned officers. Academy recruits are more nervous, have less experience (in general), and pay far more attention to what is said. There is more paperwork to do, and the setting is far more rigid, but in all, it is a far more rewarding experience to teach at an Academy. I feel a particular sense of pride when I am traveling in the area and I happened to come across one of my former students who is now a seasoned officer. I feel almost like a rock star when they recognize me and approach me to shake my hand and say hello. I do not mean to imply that everything has always gone smoothly. To be certain, there have been 'instances' over the years.

One day after the recruits had qualified, we were conducting some skill sharpening drills. One particular exercise had the student walking along the 7-yard line. The recruit would walk starting at target one and move down to target 1C where he or she would turn and walk back. The targets would be off to the student's right on the first trip, and to their left on the return. As the student walked back and forth, the range master would call out the target number, and without stopping, the student would draw fire two rounds that target and holster. On this particular day, I was range master. Officer M was functioning as the safety officer, whose job it was to watch the proceedings and stop it should any unsafe acts occur. Officer R was working as the scorekeeper. His job was to look at the targets and record the hits. The student in this case, and we three instructors had made the trip from 1 to 10 and we were on our way back. As a matter of fact, I was keeping a running total of rounds in my head and I knew there were two left in the students' magazine.

(Note: I used the word magazine here, not clip. A magazine is a device which holds rounds for a firearm. A clip belongs in a little girl's hair.)

As the student holstered his firearm after taking two shots at the designated target, I heard a muffled bang. I recognized instantly the sound of the student's firearm going off inside his holster. I knew exactly what had happened. The student, in his rush to holster, had neglected to take his finger off the trigger. As he holstered, the holster hit his finger, his finger hit the trigger, and the round went off. The next second was one of those eternity long seconds. I looked down at the ground and I counted all the boots there. Mine, the students, the safety officer, and the scorekeeper, were all without holes. I thought this was fantastic because that meant the round could only be one of two places. The most likely scenario was that it had hit the ground harmlessly and this was all just a frightening lesson for everyone. The other possibility was that the round had struck the student in the leg. By the time I had finished that thought, I heard the student groan and saw his knees buckle. We immediately took him by the arms and held them up.

He attempted to tell me that they were still rounds in his weapon. I assured him that first, the weapon had not reloaded, the action being stalled by the holster, and second, that I was neither going to let him, nor anyone touch that weapon. This recruit was a tall, muscular kid of maybe 23. He had short, cropped, blond hair, blue eyes, and in the khaki uniform recruits are required to wear, he looked a little like a propaganda photo for the Hitler youth. His height and size made it easy for us to place his arms over our shoulders and support him, as we guided him.

As we supported the student and prepared to bring him to the range shack, I glanced up the hill. Of course, as timing is everything, I saw the Academy Director stepping out of his car in the parking area near the range shack. To his credit, the director stayed out of our way and didn't question what happened until after the student was taken care of. We brought him to the range shack, placed him on a table, cut his pant leg off. An ambulance was summoned, and we inspected the wound. The entrance wound was in his upper thigh, and the path of the bullet under his muscle could be seen leading down to just above his knee. There was no exit wound. Because of

179

the trauma of such a close shot, there was minimal external bleeding. We, of course, had no idea about internal bleeding. A bandage and pressure were applied. The ambulance arrived in short order; the recruit was transported to the hospital. We explained the situation both verbally and in writing to the Academy Director. He agreed that this was an unavoidable accident and no one was at fault.

It is worth mentioning that this happened on a Thursday afternoon. On Tuesday, four days later, that recruit was in class, taking notes, participating, and even taking an exam. Whenever I feel a cold coming on or a headache and I think I might be sick for my shift, I think back to the recruit who showed up for class four days after being shot. We learned later that the bullet had traveled under his quadriceps and was lodged in his leg just above his knee. It was the decision of medical experts to leave the bullet in as it was doing no damage where it was, as the surgery to remove it would have been quite invasive. So somewhere out there one of my ex-students has a bullet in his leg. He is fortunate that he still has a leg to have a bullet in.

In addition to being nervous and anxious, some recruits are exceptionally gullible. Not all recruits are this way; some have a military background and are familiar with the functioning of firearms. The ones who enter the Academy with no experience whatsoever are easily fooled, and I will admit to having had some fun at their expense over the years. One day, while the range was being set up, I was off to the side, watching and directing the efforts of the recruits so that the range was set up to standard. While watching this happen, I had rather absentmindedly taken a loose round off the table and began to color the tip black with my sharpie marker. While I was doing this, I noted a group of young recruits watching and I could see that they were having a debate as to which of them was going to approach me and ask what I was doing.

After several pushes, and a lot of finger pointing, the young female recruit approached me. "Excuse me, sir, this recruit wishes to ask a question." She stated hesitantly while standing at rigid attention. Personally, I hate this formality and believe that the range should be a far more relaxed atmosphere. It is bad enough that I have dozens upon dozens of inexperienced people handling live firearms; I don't need them sweating the small stuff.

"Speak, recruit," I replied.

I said I didn't like the formality I didn't say that I didn't feed into it. "Sir, we were wondering what you were doing with the marker, sir." She stated as bravely as she could. She was a cute and petite young woman in her early 20s, with short black hair, and big brown eyes. She looked so innocent and trusting, I could not help myself. I could not let an opportunity to be a smartass pass me by.

"By coloring in the tip of the round like this, I effectively increase its diameter by 1 /10,000th of an inch. This allows the round to grab the rifling of the barrel earlier and puts an extra 20 to 30 spins on the round per foot. I find that all in all it tightens the grouping of my shots by at least 10%."

This is, of course, pure malarkey. Anyone with any firearms experience whatsoever knows that everything I just said makes absolutely no sense. To a recruit, however, who has just learned most of the firearms terms they will ever know this sounds reasonable. I let it go and went back to work and completed the training for the day. The following day, one of the other recruits, a man who I knew had a background as a United States Marine came up to me laughing and pointing. He was showing me that they were a group of students, about a dozen in total who had spent their afternoon the previous day coloring in the tip of every round their departments had given them. There were thousands of little colored in bullets sitting in their boxes. It must've taken them hours. The former Marine explained to me that the group had told him about what I had said, and he had backed me up. I did not have the heart to tell the recruits of their wasted time. I'm sure they have learned since then, as I am confident my name has been cursed more than a few times.

You Don't Need the Police
(But You Sure Need Help)

It is easy to assume some of what I'm telling you is untrue or at the very least exaggerated. It is not the case. While some of the stories written here may be an amalgam of different situations clustered together for an easier story, everything I've said and will say is true. Sometimes, it's hard to believe that people will call the police for the things that people call the cops for. I realize that we are the only ones up, awake and ready to handle things at that hour. But I have never understood the urgency some of the situations hold in the caller's mind.

On a Saturday morning, that is to say, a Friday night at about 2 o'clock in the morning, I received a call about illegally parked cars in a residential neighborhood. Keep in mind that 2 o'clock in the morning is when the bars close and all the drunks in the city spew out into the street at the same time. It can be a hectic hour on any day of the week, but Friday and Saturday nights are worse as you might expect. The call for illegally parked cars came with a side note that the car that was parked illegally had been there for months. Frustration and horrible thoughts popped into my head that thankfully, I was able to suppress and not say over the radio.

You mean to say that this car has been here for months, and now at 2 o'clock in the morning on a Friday night, the caller could not wait one moment more and has to have the situation rectified.

I went to the location indicated in the call. I looked over the street. I saw many cars that were parked 'illegally.' In the city, where many times each household will have multiple drivers, there is often far too few parking spaces available. People will do what they can, but it's hard to drive two blocks without seeing at least one parking violation. So I pulled out my book of parking tickets, and I tagged every car in the area indicated by the caller. Less than a minute after I pulled away from the area, dispatch received a call from the original caller saying that the officer had tagged his car along with the other vehicles. Dispatch called me and said that this man wanted to speak with me. I made my way there, and this short fat man in stained sweatpants and an old faded concert shirt demanded I take back the ticket. I asked him why he thought I would do that. He explained that since he was the caller that he should not get the ticket. I told him that that was not the rule and that if you were unhappy, he could certainly appeal the ticket.

One of the more common calls that officers get is what's known as a 'keep the peace call.' Calls of this nature are usually the result of a past domestic disturbance. One-half of the ended relationship will request police presence while going to retrieve their belongings from the residence of the other. To me, this is a very reasonable and logical thing to do. There tend to be fewer arguments or fights when a policeman is standing by. I do not question the logic of doing this at all. What I do question is the fact that almost every time I have been involved in one of these, it has been at 3 o'clock in the morning. I'm supposed to believe that this person, needs all of their clothing and stereo equipment at 3 o'clock in the morning. Often times,

184

I have had to wake up the person from whom the caller wishes to retrieve their items. I would like to think that it is simply a desperate mind working overtime and unsure what to do with themselves and the stress of a failed relationship. I know differently, however. I am aware that this is a vindictive act done to bother someone, or more likely an excuse to see if that someone had found someone new.

One morning, about 2 o'clock in the morning, I was sent to a local coffee shop. This was the days before cell phones, and the caller had actually used a pay phone in the coffee shop to request police presence in dealing with the clerk. This is a reversal of what usually happens. It is generally the clerk at the store that requires the police to deal with a customer. I arrived and spoke with my complainant. He was a young man who today might be called the hipster. He was wearing a corduroy jacket with a plaid shirt and very tight, black, 'skinny' jeans. His hair had a wild and unkempt look that I'm sure he spent hours perfecting. This young man was incensed that the clerk had refused to put his change in his hand, but had instead placed it on the counter. I retrieved the change from the counter I put it in the man's hand told him to go away because this was not a police matter. The man became increasingly angrier. He insisted that the clerk place the change in his hand. I reminded the man that he had called the police on this matter.

"Sir, whether this man wishes to touch you to give you change or he wishes to avoid that touch and places the change on the counter is not a police matter. However, your yelling, swearing, and antics have, by my estimation, disturbed the other patrons here in the store. This is a police matter as it is bordering on disturbing the peace. Would you like to go to jail? Or would you like to just get your change and go home?"

The man explained to me that I could not arrest him because he was the one that called and therefore was immune to arrest. He explained to me that I was an idiot and apparently not very good at my job. He then again demanded that the change be placed in his hand by the clerk. One last time, I grabbed the change, which was three quarters and one-dollar bill, and placed it in his hand. He threw it at me, demanding the clerk be the one to do so. I chose at that moment to challenge his 'the caller can't go to jail' rule.

I recall one woman calling the police because her sister had called her fat over the phone. This woman explained to me that she was well aware of her rights. She also knew the law and explained to me that she wanted her sister arrested. I questioned on what charge she would like her sister arrested. She looked at me as if I were the most stupid man on earth and said,

"I want her arrested for harassment. She called me fat three times. And if you do something to someone three times that is harassment "

While I had never heard harassment explained to me like that before. I told her that I would gladly write a report and that should she want to file criminal charges she was more than welcome to sign a complaint herself in court. She asked me which court she should go to, and I explained the local District Court would handle such a case. She asked which State, ours or the one her sister lives in 1500 miles away. I responded, "Either one." I walked away and actually wrote the report only because I wanted some documentation as to the ridiculousness.

There was one woman who was a thorn in my side for years. This lady was in her early 40s and had just given birth to her first child. Shortly before the birth of the child, she and her husband had purchased a home in my city, sight unseen. They had moved here from a small town in the Midwest and were unaware of the neighborhood they were to move into. I'm not saying that it was a crime-ridden neighborhood. I am saying that it bordered such neighborhoods and came as quite a shock to the young couple. In addition to the stresses that this situation caused her shortly after the birth of the child, her husband left her for reasons unknown. This woman called the police for every noise and every perceived disturbance over a two-year period. She also followed up with the complaint to the chief's office whenever the officer's response was not to her liking.

One of her chief complaints was that a homeless man was living in the park across the street from her property. I've done some research and found that she called and made this complaint over 50 times. I personally responded to more than half of those complaints. In none of the complaints that she called in regarding this homeless man was anyone ever found in the park. In one particular instance, there was fresh snow on the ground. Circling the park, I could not find a single footprint leading into or out of the park. This indicated to me, but not to her that there was no one in the park. She made a complaint specifically about me, saying that I ignored her calls and that I willingly put her and her child in danger. I was ordered to write a memo to my supervisors explaining my actions. Initially, I wrote the following.

'Sir:

The undersigned has responded to complaints of a homeless man in the park by the complaining party on numerous occasions. I have never ignored these complaints and have responded and checked on each and every occasion.

I have never once seen anyone in the park as indicated by the complainant, nor have I seen any evidence of anyone who may have left before my arrival. I would like to respectfully request a list of medications that the complainant is currently taking. Perhaps if I take the same medications, I might then see the homeless man as well.

Respectfully submitted'

Thankfully, my supervisors saw my frustration and did not accept this memo but instead had me write a less sarcastic one.

People have called the police for all sorts of problems that you would not think are police problems. I have changed fuses. I have fixed leaks, and in some cases called plumbers for people who could not accomplish even that. I have unlocked doors and climbed through windows to get people into the houses when they've locked themselves out. I've settled arguments over what television channel to watch. I have settled neighbor disputes over the overhanging branches of trees from one yard to another. It's kind of funny that in general people can't stand to have a police officer around and will question my motives if I even say hi to them on the street. Yet the very moment that anything, quite literally anything, goes wrong they pick up the phone and ask for a cruiser to be sent to them.

Someone Needs a Hug

This story takes place three days before Thanksgiving. The time of year is critical because the bitter cold plays an important role. I was in my cruiser in a parking lot near an intersection, where people ignoring stop signs have caused many accidents. I was watching the intersection while reading a variety of training updates. (Okay, it was probably comic books.) The sound of a racing engine drew my attention to a red minivan that was racing through the intersection, making a left-hand turn, and completely ignoring the Stop signs. I activated my blue lights, and the van immediately sped up. I gave pursuit and began to call off street names and direction.

The chase took me onto a highway, and into the next town over. At one point, the van spun out, and I jumped out of my cruiser, but the van recovered, and I had to jump back in to continue the pursuit. About ten minutes, maybe a little more into the pursuit I was joined by what was very likely the entire shift working in the town that the chase had led into. Very shortly after that, I received a call over the radio to disengage pursuit. The patrol lieutenant had determined that the risk of the pursuit was not justified. I acknowledged and shut off my blue lights and pulled over. I was not overly frustrated by this because I knew the road the van had just taken led to a bridge. That bridge went back to my city. I also know that that bridge was currently open to boat traffic and closed to vehicles and I

189

presumed the van be headed back my way soon. The van did not come back, but I did see multiple vehicles from the neighboring town heading for the bridge.

I called off my observations to my dispatch and made my way to the bridge. Once I arrived, I saw that the van had attempted to cross the bridge by breaking through the barriers. The bridge had not completely opened, but the barriers were across the street. Those barriers were unlike any I had seen before or since. They were large reinforced blocks of concrete on rollers that swung out into the road blocking it. The minivan destroyed the barriers, and there were chunks of broken concrete everywhere. The impact to the van had stopped it about 30 yards later. It came to rest in the middle of the bridge. Also, damage and I assume the heat from the racing engine, had caused the van to catch fire. The passenger of the van had run back into the neighboring town. The driver of the van had run forward into my city. Both of these men had police officers in pursuit.

The man who ran back into the town was quickly arrested. When I was informed of this, I went to the cruiser of the town officer who had captured him. I identified him as the man who was in the passenger seat of the minivan. I had been able to get a good look at both men when the van had spun out. The young man sitting in the cruiser was a white male in his late teens. He was wearing sweatpants and work boots and a T-shirt. He denied being in the van and stated that he was jogging. If you are going to lie to me, at least make it a good lie. It is highly unlikely that in subzero temperatures someone would be jogging at 2 o'clock in the morning dressed as he was. I noticed that he had a contusion on his forehead that was bleeding slightly. The town officer informed me that medics were on the way. I asked the terrible liar where he had hit his head to cause the apparently fresh contusion. He stated that he had run into a tree. I could see small pieces of glass protruding from the wound on his forehead. Even when I am aggravated, actually more so when I'm aggravated, I cannot help but be a smartass.

"Yes, sir, you have to be careful of those glass trees. They're tough to see at night, especially this time of year when all the leaves have fallen."

He was transported to the hospital which is in my city, and it was then that I learned what had happened to the driver. An officer from the town had chased him on foot into the city, and the driver had leaped from a pier adjacent to the bridge. He had swum under the dock, and the officer had lost sight of him. Rescue boats, rescue divers, and even Coast Guard were called out in the search for this man. That search continued for hours. Remember earlier I said to the date was important. It was bitterly cold, and this man had been in the water for hours. The search was called off. It was determined that in the morning the search would resume as a recovery rather than a rescue. As one of the last boats made its way in, an officer spotted the driver clinging to a pylon about 100 yards from where he went in.

By the time I received word of the rescue, I was at the hospital obtaining the information on the passenger. I was preparing to head to the station to start the booking and reports when I saw the ambulance crew bring the driver into the emergency room. The driver was on his back, and his arms were stretched out in front of him as though he were still hugging the pylon he was found clinging to. The ambulance crew showed me that if they brought his arms down by his side, they would return to that position. They also informed me that they were unable to obtain a body temperature on the man. The instruments available on the ambulance only record temperatures down as low as 84°F. That means that this person's core temperature was lower than that so it would not register.

Once I learn the identities of my two defendants, it came as little shock to anyone from the area. They were brothers from another neighboring town. They came from a family that was well known for generations of being car thieves. The van that they were in, and that they destroyed, was stolen from about one block from where I first saw them.

As they were both under arrest, and both in the hospital, it required officers to be hired for overtime to watch them until they could be bailed or arraigned. The damage that they did to the bridge required detail officers to be assigned to the bridge to conduct traffic operations when it opened for the next several months. Thinking on the positive side of this case, they, at the very least, made a lot of money for my brother and sister officers.

Once the booking was completed and I was at the station, I attempted to fill out the report detailing the entire series of events. The department had just upgraded to a new computer system. That system required meticulous methods of the entry of information. If you did not enter information correctly, the system would inform you that the report contained 'critical errors.' If your report had critical errors, it could not be approved, and you could not go home. It was well past ten hours since I had begun the chase. The adrenaline had worn off, and this computer was starting to anger me. Later in the book, there will be a chapter detailing technology and how it is changed from the beginning of my career. In that chapter, I will relate the story of how this report was finally turned in.

In the Long Ago
(Before Google)

When I came on this job, there were no cell phones. There were pagers also known as beepers. They were not yet common. There were of course computers, but there certainly wasn't one in every house. The Internet wasn't exactly in its infancy, but it was still a teenager. On the department, we were still handwriting reports or, if you were lucky, you got access to a manual typewriter. Yes, I said *manual* typewriter, as in *'click click click.'* I was still young enough that as technology advanced, I was able to keep up, and I learned rather quickly to adapt that new technology to my work. These days, I use Google and Facebook to find suspects. I have all the officers that I work with regularly, in my cell phone under speed dial. I do remember some of my senior officers having a difficult time adapting to new technology. I specifically remember my mother struggling. I love my mother dearly, but that did not save her from my smart-ass mouth.

When pagers/beepers first became available, I purchased one. I remember explaining several times how it worked to my mother. I would like to explain that my mother was far from a stupid person, she was in fact quite intelligent. She was however far removed from technology. I was her firstborn, and she was 40 years old when I was born. If you think about it that puts her a generation behind. I was born in the '60s, and all

193

this technology didn't pop up until the early '90s as she approached 60 years old. Her inability to grasp some of the new technology was not indicative of her intelligence. It was just a large leap forward from what she had known for 50+ years. Over and over I would explain to her that you simply had to dial the pager's number, wait for the beep, and then dial your number. Each time I would be met with an exasperated, "Oh! I can't remember that." There were a few times where she certainly did remember, but that was because she wanted to.

One day, I was in court waiting to testify. My pager went off, and I recognized my mother's number. I called, and her greeting, upon answering the phone, was these aggravated words: "They're digging in front of the house." Now, remember there were no cell phones, so I was using a landline, in the courthouse that I had begged some clerk to allow me access to. I can only imagine what the people in that office must have thought. I don't know whether or not I'm relieved that they only heard my end of the following conversation:

Ma: They are digging in front of the house.

Me: Who is digging? Is it kids? Is it dogs? What is going on?

Ma: I don't know. I think it's the city; they're digging in the street with a big machine.

Me: Well, Ma, from time to time they do that. They are probably just fixing something.

Ma: They are going to blow up the house.

(Note: There had been a news story about a week prior, about some workers hitting a gas line several towns over and destroying a house in the resulting explosion.)

Me: They are not going to blow up the house.

Ma: Yes, they are. I saw it in the news.

Me: Well, Ma. Look outside. Is there a detail officer working with the crew?

Ma: I don't know, just come here.

Me: I can't, I'm at court, and I can't just leave.

Ma: So you will go out of your way for your friends but you won't help me.

Me: I am at court, I cannot leave, and I don't know what you want me to do. If you are so concerned, just go out for a while, see a movie, go grocery shopping, just get out of the house, so it's not stressing you out.

Ma: I want you to come here.

Me: Let me get this straight. You believe the house is going to explode. Believing the house is going to explode, you would like me to be in it?

Ma: I can't talk to you. (Ma's standard conversation ended when she wasn't winning.)

When computers were introduced to the department, they were not initially a work saver. They were, in fact, the cause of some frustration. It seems that all the information had to be entered in particular ways or the computer would announce that your report had *'critical errors.'* Those critical errors were the cause of much shouting, throwing of things, heavy sighs, and various other expletives designating frustration. Admittedly, a lot of them were from me. When the system was installed, the department hired a woman to monitor the system, and she was the person to be contacted when a 'critical error' situation could not be resolved. She was so very knowledgeable of the system that she sometimes came off as arrogant. This was the cause of her not being terribly well-liked throughout the department despite the fact that she was a very pretty young lady.

Referring back to the day that I chased a minivan, and it crashed through the bridge barrier (see the previous story for the details). I had been working on the report for over two hours. The midnight shift had gone home. The day shift had arrived. Several officers had attempted to help me, but there were still many dreaded 'critical errors.' In my memories, where I am far more eloquent and self-controlled, I pushed back from the desk and sighed heavily. In reality, I probably punched the desk and swore. The computer monitor lady came over and asked what the problem was. I explained it as best I could, and she sat down and began to look over the report.

Her: See here. This is your first problem. You have the van listed as burned. That is not right.

Me: Oh yes, it is. I was there. I saw it. There were flames and everything.

Her: That may be so, but for the purposes of the report, it should be listed as stolen.

She continued to search the report and changed the van's status from burned to stolen. This action removed some but not all of the critical errors. She went to another section of the report and stopped.

Her: Okay, here you have the bridge gate down as destroyed, that is not right.

Me: Oh no but it is. See it was a gate, and now it is thousands of pieces of what used to be a gate. I assure you it is most completely destroyed.

Her: That may be so, but for the purposes of this report, it has to be listed as evidence.

Several mouse clicks and keystrokes later she changed the status of the bridge gate, and all the critical errors went away.

She looked up at me with what I thought was a rather smug expression.

Her: There, wasn't that easy?

Me: You are right that was exceptionally easy. All I had to do was tell the system that the gate that was broken into thousands of pieces was not destroyed, and the van that burned down to its very frame, as orange flames shot into the sky did not burn. Yes, you are right the system is straightforward. It is very much like a woman. You don't tell her the truth. You tell her what she wants to hear. So, thank you very much you were most kind and helpful.

I Think I Broke the Rookie

Very often, when a senior officer is given a rookie to ride with, that officer's proactivity increases. Some believe that this is because the officer is showing off for the rookie. In some cases, that might well be true. I believe, however, that more often than not is because that officer will someday be asked to evaluate that rookie, and he or she can hardly form an evaluation if nothing happens.

The very first time that I was assigned a rookie to work with turned out to be a rather eventful shift. Officer JP was a stunning young girl. She could not have been more than 22 or 23. She had blond hair pulled into a tight bun and big round blue eyes. I would be lying if I said that I did not notice the attractive shape of her athletic body. She had a high-pitched squeaky voice and an odd sense of humor that led several of my fellows to label her as 'weird.' After a few hours with her, however, I learned her idiosyncrasies and found her to be pleasant and intelligent.

On our second night working together, perhaps 20 minutes into the shift we observed a car run a red light directly in front of us. Not being used to having a partner, I grabbed the microphone and began to call off while driving and activating lights. I heard Officer JP harrumph from the passenger seat and realized that I was taking all the fun from her. The car was not stopping for my lights and siren, and I handed her the microphone to call off the chase. Okay, so giving the high-pitched squeaky voice the microphone wasn't the best option, but I was already driving it's not like we could have switched places there. The adrenaline of a new experience hit her, and she began to talk very quickly, and the pitch of her voice went up even higher than normal. The car finally pulled over several blocks later, after running two more red lights. As she called off the stop, several other cruisers arrived attracted by Officer JP's panicked voice over the radio. We all swarmed the car, and I was at the driver's window.

The driver, a skinny young man with slicked back, black hair, and pale skin was refusing to open the driver's door or even roll down the window. At one point, he shut off the car, but when he restarted it and reached for the gear shift, I had to go into action. Looking around and seeing officers all around the car I realized that if the driver was to move the vehicle, forward or back, he could've easily pinned one of my fellow officers between his vehicle and another. For the sake of the safety of everyone, I felt I had to act quickly. Removing my handcuffs from their case, I used them as brass knuckles and punched out the driver's window. Reaching in, I unlocked the door, opened it, and dragged the driver from the car before he could place it in gear. To her credit, Officer JP was immediately at my side, and together we grappled this male to the ground and cuffed him in short order. Having all those officers on scene meant that it went from chaos to order rather quickly. Each officer, in turn, offered assistance, and all the small jobs that needed to be taken care of were quickly handled.

The street supervisor arrived on the scene, it was Sergeant G, and I explained to him what had happened. At this point, Officer JP noticed that she had a long thin cut along her right inner forearm. It was evidently from a particle of glass which was embedded in the defendants' clothes, which had cut her as we grappled. The sergeant ordered her to go to the hospital and get checked out. She immediately turned to me and said, "Don't you dare write this report without me, wait till I get back." In the meantime, the sergeant looked at me and asked if I were all right. I remember as he asked me that question I was using my teeth to pull pieces of safety glass out of my left forearm. These were the little chunks of glass that auto windows tend to break into, and had become embedded in my arm when I reached through after breaking the window. I remember what a great image it must've been for me to spit out the glass and tell the sergeant that I was okay.

I finished booking the prisoner, who turned out to be a man whom I had arrested some months before. I had arrested him on the charge of impersonating an officer. He was pulling cars over, using his high beams and attempting to 'pick up' the young men he found. He was an exceptionally 'flamboyant' young man whose dress and mannerisms would cast him as the 'gay best friend' in any '80's movie. I finished booking him and I had to write the citation as that is part of the booking process. I wrote it out of Officer JP's book and affixed her number to it. I then took out a legal pad and began to jot notes to assist her in writing the report when she returned from the hospital. When she returned, her arm was heavily bandaged, and she explained that there was some difficulty in stopping the bleeding. She told me however that she was ready to write the report.

I handed her my notes and discussed with her the pattern that most police reports fall into: this is who I am, this is what I saw, this is what I did, and this is what happened as the result of what I did. She smiled and nodded her head, and I had full confidence that she could handle this. I told her that I was going to go get coffee and would check on her shortly, I even offered to buy her one. I returned about ten minutes later with coffees, and she proudly presented me her first effort. It needed a few edits. One of the first lines that needed revision, *'truly'* needed revision. She had written:

'Officer Duchesneau then became angry and punched out the window.'

I explained to her that that was not the case at all. Yes, I was angry, and yes I had punched out the window. For the purposes of the report, however, Officer Duchesneau, fearing for the safety of officers on scene, broke the window to prevent the defendant moving the vehicle. She took the criticism well. We went through the rest of the report and finished it rather easily.

The following day, I learned that Officer JP had been placed on injured status. Eventually, the cut on her arm developed an infection, which in turn produced some nerve damage. In short, that tiny little cut ended her career. I know that she was attempting to find her way back to the job when she was involved in a rather horrific motor vehicle accident. She was not killed nor permanently disabled; however, her injuries prevented her from ever being a police officer again. The running joke, among the rank, for years after was, 'Do not give Officer Duchesneau a rookie. He breaks them.'

Pretty People Go to Jail Too

One night while working uniformed patrol, I was out patrolling my area. My attention was drawn to a dark sedan which had one of its headlights out. I followed the car for a few blocks and noted a few other violations. After failing to use a turn signal and a 'rolling stop' at a stop sign, I activated my blue lights and pulled the car over. There were three people in the car, two gentleman passengers, and a young lady driving. While I was obtaining the driver's information, I noted that there were drugs and drug paraphernalia in the car. What I saw were small tight baggies of what appeared to be crack cocaine and a small glass pipe commonly used to smoke said crack cocaine.

I called for backup and had the occupants exit the vehicle to conduct a pat down for weapons. No one in the car claimed ownership of the drugs or the pipe. None of the three people in the car were the registered owner of the car. The placement of the drugs in the center console made them accessible to every person in the car. I made multiple attempts to have a reasonable conversation with these people; however, they kept their conversation cryptic and evasive. Eventually, as I could prove that no one individual possessed the drugs, I decided that all the individuals possess the drugs and I placed all three under arrest.

The two men in the car accepted the arrest, as they knew full well that they were guilty. The woman, on the other hand, made a few statements that were completely unbelievable even to my cynical and jaded ears.

"You are going to arrest me? You are going to arrest me? But look at me, I'm pretty."

I believe that her implication was that the police did not arrest pretty people. I have personally never heard of such a rule and I would be opposed to such rule's existence. In addition to this, I believe that her evaluation of her looks was somewhat exaggerated.

She was in her early 30s but looked older. She had a terrible red dye job in her hair. She was wearing a sequined halter-top that did not fit her very well. It was too tight across her belly and rather loose in the breast area. Also, the garment itself had seen better days, as it was missing several sequins. The top was rose-colored, but leaning more towards a pink hue. This, I suppose, somewhat went with her hair color. With this, she was wearing a sequined mini-skirt which was black in color. It was a different pattern of sequin, and even my untrained eye could see that it was clashing violently. I am not saying that this woman was ugly; however, I do believe she was quite far from her estimation of pretty. Perhaps at last call, after looking over the room twice for a better prospect, this woman might rate a 6 on a scale of 1 to 10. On most days and at most hours, however, I would rate her as a solid 4, perhaps a 5 with the proper grooming and dress.

21 (Don't) Jump Street

For most of my time in patrol, I was assigned to what is known as an 'early car.' What this means is that rather than arrive at midnight and attend roll call, I would arrive at 11:30 P.M., get in the car, and immediately begin responding to calls. There were several cars like this throughout the city. The purpose behind this is to eliminate a gap between shifts. If one shift goes home at midnight, and the next attends roll call for 15 or 20 minutes, the city is without an active patrol for that time. So from 11:30 P.M. until about 20 minutes past midnight, the early cars run the city.

One night, a few minutes after midnight, I was in my car taking calls when I was dispatched to a parking garage in the downtown area. The call notes were that there was a woman on the fifth floor of that garage, which is the very top. She had stepped over the restraining wall and was now standing on a 2-inch ledge looking down. The obvious implication was that she was going to jump. My mind raced with possible scenarios, as I tried to determine my best possible approach. I want to get there as quickly as possible, but I was afraid that using lights and siren would startle or spook the jumper. I had also determined that would park out of sight of the jumper and approach on foot to hopefully arrive on the fifth floor before she knew I was there. I was some distance away, approximately 2 miles, and I proceeded as quickly and safely as I could.

Officer D, who had been at roll call, thankfully heard this dispatch. The station where he was attending roll call is less than two blocks from the parking garage. He left roll call and went there ahead of me. I arrived as quickly as I could, parked the cruiser on the street, and raced up the five flights of stairs. I was betting that the adrenaline of the situation would carry me through and I would not be completely out of breath when I arrived. Thankfully, I was correct in that assumption. When I got to the top of the stairs, I saw that Officer D was standing next to the girl and holding her arm. She was still on the outside of the restraining wall. Officer D, thankfully, was inside. I will never forget the look on Officer D's face, as he saw me arrive. It was a mixture of fear and absolute gratitude. I don't think that anyone anywhere has been so happy to see me.

I looked at the girl who was refusing to make eye contact with either of us. She appeared to be of mixed heritage, but most likely a high percentage of Cape Verdean. She was about 19 years old and quite petite. I do not think she was over 5'1"; and if she was over 100 pounds, it was just barely. Shoulder short curly hair and was wearing a light jacket. At this point, I did not know what else she was wearing as that was blocked by the wall. I put a big smile on my face and attempted to talk in soft and soothing tones. I did this to try to calm our potential jumper, but I was also looking to keep Officer D calm as well. I'm not going to lie, keeping me calm was also on my agenda. I approached the two, and when I got close enough, I put my hands on the young lady's arm at wrist and elbow mirroring Officer D.

For the next several minutes, I attempted conversation with this girl. I offered her my name and asked hers. I asked what neighborhood she was from. I tried to talk about pets and family. I spoke about my pets and relatives. I did everything I could think of to engage her and put her attention on me rather than jumping. I don't know if I had any success at all. She continued to look around and refused to make eye contact or acknowledge either of us. What caused me the most concern was that she kept looking down. Each time she did this, I got the impression she was aiming. Out of the corner of my eye, I saw that Officer D was reaching behind her with his free hand. In a quick and mumbled tone, I asked him, "Have you got a hold of her pants?" Those pants, which I could now see, were rather baggie jeans, cinched tight to her waist with a studded belt.

Officer D replied, mimicking my mumbled tone, "Almost " I counted down, 3…2…1.

We each, while holding onto her arms, reached down and grabbed the belt and pulled her over the wall. Somehow, we managed to keep our feet; and working together, we handcuffed her without further incident. She did not resist and never spoke. We guided this young lady into an ambulance, and she was taken to the hospital for evaluation. We learned sometime later that she had a severe drug problem and that on that night she had taken some form of the synthetic drug. We were contacted by family members who wanted to thank us for our assistance to the fire department who had saved the young girl. The newspaper the following day credited the fire department with the lifesaving effort. I am not going to say that the firefighters were not on scene. I do remember their big red truck pulling up as we escorted the girl to the ambulance. That doesn't matter; we don't do this job for adulation.

Sometime later, we learned that this young lady was a distant relative to another officer on the department. He told us that he was appreciative of our efforts and that the young lady had a lot of problems and that he hoped that she could find help. I am sad to report that less than a year later this young lady succeeded in taking her life. I was not there, but I am told that she plunged a knife into her chest and died as a result.

Can We Keep Him?

Over the years it has become my opinion that most of the judges in my area are far too lenient. I am absolutely certain I am not the only officer to have this view. As a matter of fact, I believe that if you surveyed across the country, you would find the percentage of officers who feel that way to be very high. I have grown to understand that judges have to make decisions based on law, and law alone, and that restriction often makes them seem indifferent. I do remember, however, one day being in Superior Court, and the judge on that day was from a different area and had been brought in temporarily to fill a vacancy

While seated in the gallery, awaiting the start of my case, I watched as this visiting judge took his seat. I remember thinking that were I to cast the role of judge on a television show, this man certainly had the look. He was tall, with broad shoulders, and very stern features. His hair was mostly gray with just a hint of the black that it must've been sprinkled in. He spoke with a booming voice that was full of authority. In short, he had the look, mannerisms, and sound of what you would imagine a judge to be. He asked the clerk for each item that was to be addressed. He immediately took control of the room and proceeded to the work of the day. He had gone through several matters before my case came up. Each of these issues was handled quickly and efficiently, and I remember thinking that I liked the way this judge operated. I didn't know this at the time, but it was about to get better.

Just before my case was called, an attorney stood up and announced to the judge that his client had just arrived. His client had not been there for the earlier call. Usually, from what I have seen, a judge will simply put the matter on for a second call later in the day and handle it then. This judge was not going to waste his time like that. The judge asked the attorney why his client was late. The attorney responded that his client had gone to the wrong courthouse by mistake. The judge immediately ordered that the bailiffs take the man into custody. The judge ordered that the man be held until the end of the session when he would address the matter. The judge explained that since the man had such a difficult time finding the courthouse that he felt it best that he be secured, so he does not get lost again.

The next case to be heard was the matter that I was there on. In this particular case, I had arrested a man for an armed robbery. He had approached a woman who was exiting her car carrying both her purse and a pizza. He grabbed her from behind yanking at the purse and knocking the pizza to the ground. The young woman, who was at the time 18 years old, resisted and attempted to hold onto her purse. The robber punched her twice in the face and then grabbing her hair smashed her face into the car. This battery stunned her enough that he was able to snatch the purse away and make his escape. During this man's arrest, I spoke with him very little. He had no idea the investigation I had conducted, or what facts I knew. All he knew was that when I arrested him, there were two cards from the woman's purse in his possession. I can only imagine his surprise when he first consulted with his attorney and learned about the investigation I had conducted before my encounter with him. An investigation that included witnesses who saw him enter the area on a bicycle. Secondary witnesses informed me that they knew who usually rode that particular bike in the area and named my suspect. Surveillance footage from several nearby stores allowed me to track his movements, partially. I had, in fact, conducted an investigation that I was rather proud of. The result of all this led to a last-minute decision by the defendant and his attorney to plead guilty to the matter and take a sentencing deal offered by the district attorney's office.

Generally speaking, when a plea is changed to guilty the defendant is made to elocute to the facts of the case. When this happens, or I should say each time I've seen this happen, the district attorney will read the facts of the case aloud in court. The judge will ask the defendant if the facts that were just read are true. The defendant will answer that they are, and that will be the end of the elocution. This is not how that day's guest judge handles things. When he heard of the last-minute change, he seemed rather aggravated. I don't know if he was looking forward to a trial, or if he was just upset that the planned timing of the day was now offset. In either case, as the district attorney began to read the facts of the case, the judge stopped him. The judge asked if the victim were present in the courtroom; and if she were, he requested that she, please stand. The young lady stood, and though she had grown from the petite young girl I remembered from the night of the robbery, she was still a small and fragile-looking young lady.

The judge ordered the defendant to stand, pointed at the young lady, asking the defendant if he had punched her. He waited, and insisted that the defendant answer allowed for the record, "Yes." The judge asked if he had smashed her head into the car, and again waited and demanded the verbal

210

response. He asked lastly if the defendant had stolen that young woman's purse and when the defendant answered again in the affirmative, the judge accepted the recommendation for the change of plea. This all took place in the early afternoon of the Thursday. The defendants' attorney asked the judge for a stay of execution until the following Monday so that his client might put his affairs in order. The judge looked down at the paperwork and, seeing that the case was just shy of two years old, announced that the defendant had had plenty of time to put his affairs in order, and ordered him taken immediately into custody.

I never saw that judge again. I don't know if he ever filled in at our court again, but he never did on a day that I was there. I have not traveled much in the course of my duties and therefore have no idea what judges are like in other areas or states. I do know that compared to every judge I have ever encountered, this man was, in my opinion, fair, practical, stern, and efficient. I really wish we could have kept him.

Sometimes You Don't Win

Looking back at some of the stories that I've written so far, I've noticed or rather it was brought to my attention that in each story I came out on top, or at the very least I got the last word in. I asked my friend to look over what I had written, and he brought to my attention that the collection of stories seemed a little bit like bragging. I justified this by saying, "Well, those are the stories which pop most quickly to memory. Those are the funniest stories." He looked at me and nodded. He then gave me a look that told me he was about to call me on my bullshit.

"I know full well you remember the failures," he said, "and why does the story have to be funny?" He was right of course; I remember the failures. No one says it has to be funny. I can't help myself I have a smart mouth and I will always go for the joke if I can. In this next story, I couldn't.

One morning at just about daybreak, in the middle of winter, I was dispatched to assist Officer A. She is an excellent young officer, who at the time had about two years on the job. She is a very pretty blond girl, of Eastern European descent. She has a great accent, is well above average intelligence, and has the right instincts for this job. The call I was to assist her on was a medical call. The notes to the call were the ones that I believe every officer dreads.

"Infant not breathing; CPR instructions being given over the phone."

I arrived seconds behind Officer A. As I exited my cruiser, I saw her walking up the stairs, carrying her medical bag and AED. I followed right behind her. In the house, we were met by a variety of adults and children. We were pulled, pushed, and directed to a back bedroom where an infant of about two months was lying face up on the bed. The bed was in a small bedroom that was so cluttered with toys and clothes and papers that there was barely room to maneuver. I grabbed the bag from Officer A and knelt behind her while she attended to the infant. I saw her check for a brachial pulse, and she shouted back, "No pulse!"

I broke the seal on the medical bag, and a fixed the smallest mask to the oxygen line. I slapped Officer A on the left leg. Without us ever having discussed it, when I did that her left hand shot backward open and ready to grab whatever I was handing up. I placed the mask her hand and told her, "Oxygen, flowing." She fixed the mask to the child while I broke out the ampoule bag. This is a bag that is squeezed by the emergency responder to give a flow of air and avoid mouth-to-mouth contact. Again, I slapped her leg, and again she reached back to receive the equipment. I named it as I handed it to her. Throughout this, she continued CPR, and I broke out and set up the AED. By the time the AED was affixed to the infant, the firefighters and EMTs had arrived. We handed over the care of the infant to them and began to secure the scene.

I called for a street supervisor and informed him that he would likely have to call detectives as I did not believe that the child would survive. I, of course, did not make the statements within earshot of any family member. Officer A and I began to record the names of all persons present along with very brief statements as to where they were, where the baby was, what they were doing. I won't go into details, but the parents of the child had evidently been sleeping in the bed together with the child. Their movement in sleep coupled with the variety of blankets, pillows, and laundry on the bed had been a lethal combination. It appeared that the child was accidentally smothered.

As you can well imagine, there were quite a bit of hysterics in the house. One of the things that they do not teach you in the Academy, as it cannot be taught, is how to remain calm when the world around you has dissolved into chaos, and all you want to do was scream. I did my very best. I flipped the switch in my brain and shut off everything that was my personal self. It left my training, it left my instincts, but I shut down the parts that make me, me. I have no children, but I know that Officer A does. I observed her, and she mimicked me and went right about her job. I remember afterward being very proud of her. I told her to escort the parents to the hospital. I told her that I would stand by at the house for the supervisor and detectives. She packed up the hysterical, teenaged parents and got them to the hospital behind the medics. Without being told she even delayed things to give the medics time to arrive and get the baby into the emergency room so that the parents didn't have to see that. Officer A is truly an exceptional officer.

While attempting to complete the list of people in the house, and doing it without sounding accusatory, I was approached by a little girl of about six years old. She tugged on my sleeve, and standing there in her little green footy pajamas clutching a blanket, she asked, "Is the baby going to be dead?" I had no idea what to say. On the one hand, I absolutely hate lying. I especially hate it when dressed in the uniform. I do not wish to be the officer who lied, in the memory of any child. In this instance, however, I did not have the courage to tell this child the truth. It struck me that the baby

214

was so young that the child was not even sure of the name and merely referred to her as 'the baby.' I told her that the baby was going to the hospital and that the doctors would help her. I could argue that that wasn't exactly a lie. I could claim that I do not have a medical degree and therefore could not be sure of the outcome, so what I said may not have been a lie. If I am, to be honest with myself, however, I knew full well that that baby was going to die. I just did not have the bravery to be the man who told her big sister.

I have now stared at, and reread the previous paragraph four times. I know why. It's because I don't want to write what comes next. For all my bluster, and all the times that I have shrugged off fear, insult, and injury; I find it very hard to write the words, 'The baby died.' The scene was turned over to detectives. Officer A and I wrote initial reports and went home.

This case bothers me; it bothered me openly for a long time. It still bothers me. I just hide it a little better every day. We did everything right. We were great at our job that day. Officer A and I functioned as though we had practiced 1000 times. The baby died anyway. When you do everything right, you're supposed to win. Sometimes, you don't win.

The Wheels on the Bus

As I have mentioned before, I absolutely hate working details that involve directing traffic. The inattention that the average driver has regarding the world around them frightens and frustrates me. It has taken me hours to mentally and emotionally 'come down' after working some jobs. Because of this, I have often sought out paid details that were not traffic related. For a period of time, the local bus terminal hired police officers to work a detail there. The primary responsibility of those officers was to keep order in and around the terminal. It mostly consisted of removing smokers from the non-smoking areas, removing loiterers, and generally enforcing the rules of the terminal. I found that it also included assisting junkies who had overdosed in the bathrooms, settling petty arguments between the staff and patrons, and witnessing the monumental stupidity of which human beings are capable. I like this job mostly because it comes very close to resembling actual police work. The terminal and its property take up most of a city block. To me, it is like walking the world's smallest beat. It is a beat. However, that encompasses people from all over the city, so it becomes a small model of my city contained within that city block.

Smoking within the building of the terminal is prohibited. This part is usually a non-issue. Smoking is also banned in any of the waiting areas, where buses pick up and drop off passengers. This has been the focal point of more than a few arguments. I have found that when I approach someone who is smoking in one of these areas, one of three things will happen.

The first, and by far the least common, reaction I get when I tell someone that they are in a non-smoking area and ask them to remove themselves with their lit cigarette is what a reasonable person would expect. They will look around; realize where they are and what they are doing. They will then immediately snuff out their cigarette. They usually apologize, and either figure the situation out for themselves and walk outside or ask me where they would be allowed to smoke and then move there. This is as I said the least common reaction I have received.

The second, for some reason, involves motion. It also, for some reason, generally includes the words 'I'm just.' I will often observe people walking through the waiting area while smoking a cigarette. I will attempt to correct them on this and tell them that this is a non-smoking area. They will then offer me excuses that four times out of five contain the words 'I'm just.' Some examples:

"I'm just walking through."

"I'm just seeing if that is my bus."

"I'm just heading out there now."

I recall one woman who was just about to light her cigarette when I stopped her and pointed out that she was in a non-smoking area. Specifically, I pointed out that she was standing directly under a sign prohibiting smoking. I did this rather politely, but admittedly some of my innate sarcasm probably snuck through. This young woman, who was probably not yet 25, turned from me without a word and began to walk out to the sidewalk. Before she had walked 5 feet, she lit the cigarette. I stopped her and questioned her motives. Did she not understand me? Was she purposely disrespectful? Was

217

her short-term memory so bad that she had already forgotten our conversation? I asked her all these questions, and again I probably did a poor job of disguising my contempt and sarcasm.

"Did you not see me walking as I lit the cigarette?" she asked, as if the act of walking somehow negated her smoking within the waiting area. I asked her, admittedly with a raised voice and absolutely no attempt to hide my frustration, what walking had to do with the entire situation. She reiterated that she was walking, and mentioned that I had no right to raise my voice to her. I told her that I was wearing my hat.

The third reaction is anger, instant and unwarranted anger. One man, who was leaning against the wall while smoking, informed me that if I was going to enforce a no smoking rule, signs should be put up. When I pointed out that his head was less than 3 inches from the G on the no smoking sign, he stepped back and looked the sign over. He then flicked the cigarette at my feet and noted that the sign also listed 'no standing' and 'no soliciting.' He then asked if I were going to arrest him for standing because he was also standing. The loud, aggressive, and challenging manner in which he asked me this prompted me to in fact place him under arrest for the disorderly conduct and disturbance he was causing. I didn't tell him that, I told him he was under arrest for standing.

In addition to the smoking and loitering issues, I occasionally have to deal with a car or bicycle riding through the terminal. This is exceptionally dangerous, as the buses are not expecting small vehicles to be on their track as they go through the terminal. Buses, being rather large vehicles, are not designed to nor can they stop on a dime. It is doubtful that a surprised bus driver could stop in time to avoid a bicyclist they were not expecting. Here, as with the no smoking issues, the 'I'm just' excuses seem to fly. As I stop a car from turning into the terminal, as it passes under the giant 'BUSES ONLY' sign, I am inevitably met with an 'I'm just' excuse. They are either just dropping someone off, or picking someone up. They don't believe that the rule applies to them because they're only violating it a little. They are just doing whatever they need to do, and once that's over, they will gladly follow the rules again. See, once again a detail involving motorists is driving me angry. Cars are not the only issue; bicyclists also try to ride through the terminal. I have to ask six or more persons a day to get off, and walk their bike, and not on the track where the buses travel. Most react in one of two ways. They either do as I asked, or ignore me altogether and continue their trip through the terminal. Thankfully, as of this time, I have had no accidents or injuries. One gentleman while going through the terminal stuck in my mind for a variety of reasons. To that gentleman, I post this as an open letter. Sir, if you read this someday and you'd know who you are, please feel free to look me up.

An open letter to the man on the lavender bike

'Sir,

One day as you rode your lavender bicycle East through the bus terminal I was the officer working that day. I asked you to please get off your bicycle and walk it through, outside of the bus tracks so you would not be struck. You continued to ride and extend your left hand toward me raising your middle finger in what I perceived as your attempt to engage in conversation. Unfortunately, I was unable to catch up with you on foot. I am a bit confused because by raising your middle finger you seemed to be attempting to start a conversation.

Your follow-up actions however when you noticed I was running toward you indicated you wanted to avoid a conversation with me. You wheeled through traffic, and picked up speed, making it impossible for me to continue a foot pursuit. If in fact, you wish to be a brave man and someday pursue this conversation with both of us on foot, face-to-face and man-to-man, I will gladly meet you at that bus terminal where we can discuss a quiet place where our conversation will not be interrupted.

    Respectfully;

    Ofc. N. Duchesneau'

There are often times where absolutely nothing will happen during a bus terminal detail. These days are rare, but they do happen. There are times however when events occur which challenge my ability to process stupidity. I recall one summer day where my attention was drawn to three young girls, who had cornered and were yelling at a fourth young girl. Approaching the situation, and asking what was going on, I noted that the three young girls yelling were all black, and the recipient of their verbal tirade was white. I further noted that all four girls seemed to be of high school age. As I asked what the problem was, all three of the angry young girls turned on me and began to make me the focus of their anger. They noted out loud that I, being a white officer, would probably do nothing. They informed me that instead of killing black people I should be doing something about the offensive nature of this girl's shirt. I was initially taken aback by the absolute viciousness that these three young women turned on me with. As I looked beyond them to the scared young girl in the corner, who had up until that moment been the target of their anger I saw that she was wearing a rather generic 'Who' T-shirt. The front of the shirt in addition to the band's name was emblazoned with the shape of Great Britain. Superimposed upon the form was the Union, Jack. Initially, I could not understand what these women thought was so offensive about the shirt.

"Offensive to who, Rush fans?" I asked as I could not understand why a concert shirt would be offensive.

As all three women were talking at once, it was difficult to make out what they were saying. Mostly, they were directly accusing me of taking the offensive woman's side because we were both Caucasian. I did note that several times in their tirade the phrase 'that flag' was used. I suddenly realized what was going on. These rather uneducated women, who were so eager to find something to be offended by, had confused the Union Jack with the Confederate battle flag.

I offered the following bit of advice. "That is the Union Jack. It is the flag of Great Britain because the band that T-shirt represents is a British band. It is not the Confederate battle flag, and in reality, does not resemble it in the slightest. I suggest that you spend far more time seeking an education than being offended by the world."

I am told that these women made a complaint regarding my response to my department's internal affairs division. I am further told that they were laughed out of the office.

One day, I was keeping my eye on one particular man. He was wondering around and in and out of the bus terminal for hours. He gave no indication that he was waiting to board a bus, or that he was waiting for someone to arrive by bus. He did, however, show all signs of being intoxicated. His mannerisms and the way he walked led me to believe that on this hot summer day he had reached an impressive level of intoxication before noon. As I watched him enter the building for the third time, I was about to approach him and tell him to find someplace else to be. I saw him look up at the illuminated 'occupied' sign above the men's room. He then walked out of the building and leaned against the large window that made up the northern wall. As I walked outside to tell him to move along, I saw that he was urinating in his pants and down his leg. Very soon, he was standing in a large puddle of urine. I saw that several women and children in the area witnessed this and were repulsed by it. When the flow of urine had stopped, I approached the man, and he immediately began to yell at me saying:

"What, are you going to arrest me for pissing? You can't arrest me; I never whipped it out."

I informed the man that I agreed with the fact that he had not, in fact, exposed his penis to the world; however, it was my opinion that his actions were disorderly and amounted to a breach of the peace, and so I chose to challenge his defense that he could not be arrested.

Good Times

Not every encounter with people is a negative, although it sometimes seems that way. There have been many wonderful events in my time as a policeman. I've met some truly wonderful people who have brightened my day with the tiniest of effort. I wish that I could properly thank them all, but there really is no way to get that done. It is my hope that by mentioning them here, they will somehow remember their encounter with me and know that they made a difference.

At the end of my shift one day, I walked over to a coffee shop to fuel up for a second shift. Actually, I believe that day I was heading to a paid detail directing traffic. I was tired, and my mood was sour because I honestly do hate directing traffic. I was still in uniform naturally. As the coffee shop is less than a block from the station, it was an easy stop before retrieving my car and heading off to the next job. A young boy of about six or seven years old got my attention by tugging on my sleeve. I looked down to see his little smiling face peering up at me. I could not at the time nor can I now imagine a bigger smile.

"Well, hello there, and what's your name?"

He did not respond but only made a small 'squeak' sound and continued to grin. His mother walked up and apologized for him bothering me. I replied that he was no bother at all and again asked the young man his name. His mother told me that his name was Jake and that Jake couldn't talk. She said that he was autistic and had not learned to speak (yet). She explained that Jake absolutely loves police officers and gets very excited when he sees one. I looked down at this joyous child with his short blond hair, and huge green eyes, proudly displaying a mouthful of widely spaced teeth. I presented him my hand and shook his firmly telling him that it was my great pleasure to meet him. I retrieved my coffee and headed out the door, as mother and son returned to the table. As I exited the door walking past the table, I looked down to see Jake taking a huge bite from a chocolate donut.

"Bye, Jake, have a great day," I said, waving enthusiastically at the young boy.

"Wow, Jakey, the officer remembered your name. Isn't that cool?" Jake's mom said.

I absolutely love that encounter. The fact that I could make that young boy so happy simply by acknowledging him was very empowering.

While working in detectives, I was given the case involving a housebreak. During that housebreak, the only thing stolen was a rather old and expensive Tiffany lamp. The victim in this housebreak was a woman in her 90s. She was mentally quite sharp, though physically she had difficulty in getting around. This was a rather simple case, as the initial interview with her revealed that her grandson had visited her 'out of the blue,' just days before the break. Quickly, researching the local pawnshops and searching for this man's name, I was able to determine that he had, in fact, sold the lamp at one of the stores the same day as the break. I was able to retrieve the lamp from the shop and return it to the victim. This lamp was very important to her as it had been a gift from her grandmother, and she had had it for a long, long time. She was so delighted to get her lamp back that she burst into tears. I have a very vivid memory of her telling me thank you over and over again, and she said that she wanted my name. I gave her my name, and she very carefully wrote it down in a little notebook she kept near her sofa. She informed me that I would be added to her prayers every night. I count this as one of the best interactions I have ever had with someone on the job.

As I have mentioned before, I have for a long time been a fan of professional wrestling. I know the storylines and their characters very well. (Yes, I know it's fake. You don't have to tell me. By the way, Santa Claus is fake too.) One day, while walking the beat in the downtown area, I was approached by two young men in their teens. Each of them was wearing a T-shirt emblazoned with a different professional wrestler. I noted that both wrestlers were from an era of 12 or 15 years previous. I had to make mention of this, and I said, "Cool shirts, boys." This attracted their attention, and they walked over to greet me. It was at this point that I noted that both young men had some type of disability. I think it may have been autism or some variant thereof, but I can't be sure. Regardless of this, both young men were elated to be noticed. An older man who was with them and apparently a caretaker of some sort smiled and waved at me, as I spoke with them. We talked about wrestling for a few minutes, and I listened as each boy, in turn, told me their favorite wrestler, and imitated their interview styles.

Realizing that I was wearing a police uniform and that in it I bore a strong resemblance to a wrestler known as 'The Big Boss Man,' I shouted out his tagline as the boys walked away.

"You better watch yourselves or you will be doing *hard time!*"

I knew from the look on their faces that I had friends for life.

Over the years, I have arrested many dangerous criminals. I've saved lives. I have changed lives for the better and worse. I have been to places where my mere presence has made the difference between disaster and success. Having all these things in mind, I still count these small encounters as some of my very favorite moments on the job.

Cast

Officer T: An Academy mate of mine. He is one or two years older than me. A dark-haired, blue-eyed Frenchman about 6 foot tall. A brilliant man with a talent for technology.

Officer S: One of the best officers I know. At about 6 foot 2, he is in fantastic shape and works hard to stay that way. He's quick-witted and knows the job very well. He doesn't just know the laws and rules but how to best apply them as well.

Officer A: A young officer who I had the pleasure of assisting in training. She and her family originally come from Eastern Europe, and she has a delightful accent. She is much smarter than I could hope to be. And though I make a joke about her being my replacement, I secretly believe that's true.

Officer G: Another Academy mate of mine. We've known each other since we were about 12 years old. Our mothers were good friends, and though we didn't spend an enormous amount of time together as children, we have known each other for more than 40 years. He is a very smart athletic man, with what might be considered a twisted sense of humor.

Officer D: An officer of about 12 years my junior. I've had the pleasure of working with him from the time he was fresh out of the Academy to a point where he was considered one of the senior men of the relief. By far one of the funniest people I know. His humor is dry, but once you 'get' him, he's hysterical. Heavyset blond and blue-eyed. While not very tall, he is a force to be reckoned with. When he yells, even I jump. He has that kind of inherent authority.

Officer JP: A young female officer who was only with the department for a brief time. She is a beautiful girl with blond hair and blue eyes. She has a very attractive body and an odd sense of humor. She has a high-pitched voice which was often the point of some teasing.

Sergeant J: A brilliant woman with more than 35 years of experience in law enforcement. An absolutely no-nonsense supervisor who I initially feared as a rookie and now count amongst my friends. She is a slight build and small stature and quite potentially one of the most dangerous people in the department. As defensive tactics and firearms instructor, she knows countless ways to hurt you.

www.ingramcontent.com/pod-product-compliance
Lightning Source LLC
LaVergne TN
LVHW051626080426
835511LV00016B/2194